Petticoat Surgeon

The Extraordinary Life of Dr. Bertha Van Hoosen

MAUREEN THALMANN

In the
Fullness
of Time

ISBN: 0692302387
ISBN 13: 9780692302385
Library of Congress Control Number: 2014917449
In the Fullness of Time, Oakland, MI

For Rick, the hero in the story of my life.

Contents

Foreword

⸻⸻

Maureen Thalmann carefully documents and introduces us to a remarkable woman: Dr. Bertha Van Hoosen. Her research allows us to meet a gifted doctor, teacher, and philanthropist as well as a woman deeply connected to her upbringing on the Van Hoosen Farm and to her family.

Dr. Van Hoosen was a determined supporter of the cause that women deserve an equal opportunity in the medical field. In this book, you will meet a person who is an exceptional inspiration. Her determination to being an honest, ethical, highly skilled doctor, while overcoming myriad obstacles in her career, will provide life lessons to every reader. Maureen Thalmann's research and writing allow us to stand next to Bertha in the operating room or at her desk late at night and to peek into the life of one the greatest Americans in the field of medicine.

Patrick McKay, Director
Rochester Hills Museum at Van Hoosen Farm

Introduction

———✺———

At the time of her death in 1952, Bertha Van Hoosen was the oldest practicing, and one of the best-known, physicians of her era. Over half a century later, this Michigan native's life and accomplishments are largely unknown to the general public. Van Hoosen is honored by members of the American Medical Women's Association (AMWA), the organization she founded in 1915 to serve as a voice for fellow female physicians and to increase the number of female doctors through scholarship and internship opportunities. Academic readers find Van Hoosen referenced in scholarly articles and publications about pioneering female physicians and the history of childbirth in the United States. Her story is shared with local visitors to the historic house museum in Oakland County that was once her home, but other than her 1949 bestselling autobiography *Petticoat Surgeon*, there has been no comprehensive biography of this medical trailblazer. In writing this book, I hope to tell this outstanding woman's story. I look at the influences that created the focused, driven woman who left home to pursue a medical career and earned a reputation as a leader in the struggle for equality in the medical profession.

Born the younger of two daughters on a southeast Michigan farm, nature was Bertha's earliest teacher as she accompanied her adored father on his agricultural chores. Joshua Van Hoosen was a man ahead of his time. Hardworking and successful, he saw the day when his daughters would need as much education as any young man, and he sought to give them every opportunity he could. His example of personal sacrifice and diligent labor helped his daughter forge a life of accomplishment, adventure, and compassion for others within the confines of a society that had not yet accepted women's active participation.

When fate took the men of the family to early graves, Bertha became the head of a unique female nuclear family that supported her through her demanding career, and it offered the shelter and emotional bond that the unmarried physician needed. Her career spanned the eras of horse-and-buggy transportation and jet air travel, and her many letters and professional papers document the changing world and the place of women in it. I hope to reintroduce this fascinating woman to modern readers, encourage an appreciation of her accomplishments, and humanize the woman behind them.

I am grateful to the staff of the Chicago History Museum, the University of Chicago Archives, the Bentley Historical Library at the University of Michigan–Ann Arbor, and the AMWA archives housed at Drexel University in Philadelphia for their assistance in sorting through Van Hoosen's extensive papers. My greatest debt goes to Patrick McKay, the supervisor of interpretive services at the Rochester Hills Museum at Van Hoosen Farm for generous access to the museum's archives and for his great encouragement and friendship.

ONE

The Farm, a Refuge in Almost Any Storm

———✦———

Sarah Van Hoosen Jones relaxed in front of the crackling fire. She was pleased to be home, but it had been a bittersweet return. Her beloved grandmother had died, and the young woman had traveled from Chicago to prepare the small house for its mistress's final homecoming. The house appeared just as Grandmother had left it. The only change was the photo of Grandmother that Sarah had hung over the parrot's cage. Sarah looked at the photo now; it was of Grandmother at age eighty-eight, her face showing the cares of a long life. Small in stature, like Sarah, Grandmother stood next to the silos added to the farm's 1874 barn. She wore a black dress as she had every day since losing her husband of forty-one years, Joshua, twenty-seven years ago.

Sarah felt a connection to Grandmother, one that transcended family ties. Theirs was a shared love for this farm. They found contentment on the land and among their friends in the village of Stoney Creek. Grandmother had spent a quiet life reading the Bible as Sarah sought inspiration in the science of nature. While her own daughters had sought lives far from this tranquil corner of Michigan, Grandmother found fulfillment among the gently rolling hills and whispering creeks of their family's land. Her oldest daughter left home to pursue a career as a teacher, and she loved the culture and entertainment that a large city offered. Her younger daughter, Bertha, had answered a call to serve in the field of medicine, and her profession took her far beyond the enclave that was their home. Sarah found the same contentment that her grandmother had. At age twenty-nine, a new life stretched before her. Her grandmother had assured that the farm that had been her refuge would now be Sarah's home.

1

The farm was three hundred acres of fertile soil in Avon Township, Michigan. Crossed by dancing streams, the territory was an unspoiled wilderness when Sarah's maternal great-grandfather, Elisha Taylor, left New York State to survey the land his father bought in 1823 for one and a quarter dollars per acre. The family moved the following year. Forty-four family members made the arduous three-month trek via the Erie Canal and around Lake Erie through Cleveland and Detroit. They were greeted by the inhabitants of a few log cabins in Rochester before cutting their way through virgin forests to high ground. Below, they saw a welcoming home site in a peaceful valley. The hills surrounding the valley offered natural protection from the wind. Springs of cold, clear water ran down the sides of the hills and into a creek that ebbed its way through the property.

A few years after their arrival, the Taylor clan had created a thriving village that consisted of a church, a school, a tavern, a smithy shop, and mills. The Taylors were millwrights, and it was the pulsing creeks that had attracted them to this land. The air filled with the sound of wood mill wheels turning to the power of the rushing water. By 1876, the village held two woolen mills and two cider mills. Grandmother, Sarah Taylor, was born into this thriving pioneer community in 1830. The fifth of seven children, Sarah grew up surrounded by family. She was involved in the day-to-day activities of home and mill and educated in a one-room schoolhouse.

In that schoolhouse, Sarah met six-year-old Joshua Van Hoosen. Also born in 1830, Joshua's family had migrated from Canada six years later. His Dutch-born father and American mother had eleven children and little money on their arrival at Stoney Creek. Mrs. Van Hoosen was the daughter of a Tory, an American who took the side of the British during the Revolutionary War and escaped to Canada as the new nation was founded. Lacking ambition, the senior Joshua Van Hoosen kept his family in a state of poverty as the Taylors of Stoney Creek prospered around them. Mrs. Van Hoosen's granddaughter later reported that she had to work on "almost nothing a year" to keep "the wolf from the door of her ever-increasing family."

Young Joshua rebelled against the family's financial condition and found employment as a child. He picked thorns from hawthorn bushes to be used in lieu of pins to close the sacks of wool at the Taylor mills. At age ten, Joshua worked in a store owned by a church deacon whose dishonest business practices turned Joshua away from established religion. Frustrated by his family's poverty and eager to strike out on his own, the fourteen-year-old approached his father with the idea of purchasing his time until he was twenty-one and freeing himself from responsibility to his parents. The young man proposed that if his father would buy a farm, he would help pay for it and care for his parents, but the younger Van Hoosen must hold the deed. Or, young Joshua suggested, "I'd pay you one hundred dollars for my time until I am twenty-one." When his father agreed to being paid for his son's time, Joshua found work splitting rails and was able to work off his indebtedness by age eighteen. Eager to be a landowner, he worked as a day laborer with a local farmer and eventually formed a land-purchase partnership with the man.

The exuberant, red-headed six-footer was an unlikely companion for the demure Sarah Taylor. She developed a lifelong love of education and became a teacher. Small and serious, Sarah was never known to joke, and her demeanor was as different from Joshua's as her dark eyes were from his steel-blue ones. While her family disapproved of the relationship, Joshua's life plans revolved around the purchase of land and his life with Sarah.

Learning of the discovery of gold in California during the summer of 1848, Joshua's life changed. He sped up the process of acquiring land by traveling to the West Coast to mine for gold. He left Stoney Creek in November 1851. Taking the safer, shorter route meant traveling to New York City. In the bustling metropolis, the youth was immediately taken for a "country bumpkin" according to his daughter. He was targeted by a group of hooligans eager to relieve him of his "belly belt" filled with his savings. Joshua later told his daughter that he did not feel safe until he was in his bunk aboard the ship to Nicaragua. After crossing Nicaragua in a wagon, Joshua boarded another ship bound for San Francisco, and he arrived there in January 1852. Following the Sacramento River, he joined other gold seekers in the community of Rough and Ready.

Letters crossed the continent. One letter from Joshua contained a marriage proposal and a gold nugget for making a ring. Sarah coyly responded that although she could not answer the proposal, she liked no "other boy" better than him. A Stoney Creek friend wrote Joshua that his "little black-eyed girl was lively and in good spirits and wearing on her finger some of the gold of California."

Joshua returned in the fall of 1853, carrying the fruits of his labor in a belt pack. He used the gold to buy property, and his first major land purchase was a hill south of Stoney Creek Village. He married Sarah on January 1, 1854, in her sister's Stoney Creek home. The couple's first child, Alice, was born there in 1855. Following Alice's birth, the Van Hoosens moved to a rented house in the village proper.

The new property was heavily wooded and required clearing before the crops could be planted. Hired hands helped Joshua in pulling stumps and planting, and Alice became her mother's helper and companion at home. While Joshua could be found in the evenings congregating with local men on the steps of the village store, Sarah concentrated on her family. She shared her love of reading with her young daughter who could read the newspaper and Bible by age five.

In 1863, Joshua was teased by the village men for fathering a second daughter, Bertha. Eight-year-old Alice rejoiced in her sister's birth and ran to her grandmother's home in the village to share the good news. Adored by their parents and watched over by family, neighbors and farm help, the Van Hoosen children were oblivious to the storm of war raging around them. Only Joshua's status as a resident alien kept him from the front lines of the Civil War. Family members wrote to Joshua, asking for help to buy their way out of military service. His responses did not survive.

After the death of Sarah's mother in 1864, Joshua bought out the other heirs and took over the Taylor family homestead. The home the young family moved into was the 1840 Taylor farmhouse. It was a small-frame residence, a story and a half high with two rooms downstairs and three on the second floor. Joshua added a dining room, kitchen, additional bedroom, pantry, summer kitchen, and woodshed, all rambling to the west and north of the original structure. The front of the house faced south, overlooking the stream and Mount Moriah. Joshua added a wide porch supported by wood posts with green shutters at the windows to block the summer sun and heat.

Sarah became the only village woman with running water at her door when Joshua created a system that brought clear spring water to the house from the hills beyond the creek. He cut tamarack trees and bore holes through them to construct a length of log pipe. Explaining to doubting neighbors that "water will always seek its level," his pipes carried water from the spring down the hill, under the creek, and up a small hill to the house. He had running water for the horse barn, a roadside trough, and the dairy barn. The roadside trough became a gathering place for the exchange of political thought and neighborhood gossip. Bertha wrote of a fountain, a cement basin with the whirling spray of a lawn sprinkler in the middle that attracted attention to the farm's front yard and provided salmon for Stoney Creek. Sarah convinced her husband to create a semi-indoor toilet facility by cutting a door between the home's woodshed and the outhouse on the other side of the woodshed's wall.

In 1865, Joshua retired his farm mortgage and celebrated by purchasing sheep and shorthorn cattle. Life for the Van Hoosens followed the rhythm of the era's subsistence farmers: planting, cultivating, and harvesting crops. Joshua's trips to Detroit to market his produce took two days over corduroy roads. There were sheep to be shorn, pigs to be butchered, an icehouse to pack with ice and fish, and walnuts and hickory nuts to be harvested.

Joshua's helpmate in his chores on the farm was his second daughter, Bertha, who later described herself as the "doglike companion" of her father. Physically similar to her father, she earned the nickname "Ginger" due to her red hair and "hot baby temper." At planting time, the sturdy girl followed her father, dropping corn kernels into the holes that he dug. Their friendly competition at husking time found her trying to work faster than her father with the husking peg he made especially for her. In summer, she sat on a fence watching him work the mowing machine and waiting with a pail of ice water for each of his turns past her. Bertha had a childhood "carefree as Pan." She reported that for her first sixteen years, she roamed the fields "barefooted and bareheaded when weather permitted." As an adult, she said the farm lay the "groundwork for her physical resistance" and was the "solar plexus of the family."

Life on the farm did not shelter her from the cadence of life and death. With reproduction a necessity in rural life, farm children were never sheltered from the facts of life. "Production and reproduction is the rural theme that marks the time and synchronizes everything on a farm," Bertha wrote. The visits of neighborhood stallions and bulls were never secretive, and the knowledge of sex came early. Finding a knothole to view the activity in the barn, young Bertha viewed the flirtation of a visiting stallion and an unwilling mare. Watching the strange behavior of the farm's cows as they came into heat and their subsequent visit to a neighbor's bull helped her put together the puzzle of reproduction. The first time she witnessed a birth was when her pet cat gained an unusual amount of weight and then found a nesting place in the family's woodpile. Perching above where the cat lay, she watched five glistening kittens enter the world and be vigorously cleaned by their mother. When the daughter of a neighboring farmer offered to share the secret of where babies came from, Bertha was indignant that the girl should think she was ignorant of such things. Her retort was "I have always known."

The future surgeon related that her first lesson in anatomy, her favorite subject, was "begun in the back yard at hog-killing time." Watching the process from the sharpening of the knives and axes to the conversion of the carcasses into hams, tenderloins, ribs, and other byproducts, Bertha "reveled in seeing what was under the skin." Learning to dress chickens and turkey continued her education.

Life on the Van Hoosen farm taught self-reliance. "When I wanted playthings, I made them—boats whittled out of scraps of wood," toys "cut from pumpkins," and dolls' clothing from remnants left from her mother's sewing. For companions, she had her choice of farm animals and a three-hundred-acre farm as an unrestricted playground.

Eight years older and physically more like her mother, Alice gave her sister her first lessons in botany and horticulture. The sisters knew the location of all the flora and fauna that covered the countryside around their home. Alice taught Bertha to press and dry wild flowers and to create a collection of bird's eggs by blowing out their contents through a pinhole. They caught insects with a net and killed and mounted butterflies and beetles on pins. Alice taught Bertha the scientific names for their collections, names Bertha never forgot.

The sisters' temperaments were as different as their looks. Alice was petite and fine featured with dark hair and eyes. Bertha was a sturdy child with "copper-colored locks, twisted into soft curls" and steel-blue eyes like her father's. Bertha described their personalities in the terms of the Hippocratic temperaments. She described her younger self as "phlegmatic, unruffled, calm, and sluggish," while Alice was self-conscious and temperamental. Despite the differences in their personalities and ages, the sisters developed a close bond. Their mother never allowed them to argue even though Alice's self-consciousness sometimes caused her embarrassment over Bertha's self-absorbed, plodding ways. Alice's relationship with her younger sister was almost maternal and always affectionate. Bertha remembered only one serious spat. Alice lost patience with her younger sister's lack of effort on a shared chore. After correcting Bertha several times, Alice slapped the six-year-old in frustration. Deciding that letting the insult pass might lead to repetition, Bertha struck her older sister with "as near a Joe Louis return" as she was able. Stunned more than hurt, Alice and Bertha both broke into tears and never let the episode repeat.

Sarah ran an organized but plain home. Bertha remembered spending time at the home of Aunt Electa, her mother's oldest sister and the Van Hoosen's neighbor. Aunt Electa's home was filled with homemade decorations: wreaths of flowers made of hair, frames decorated with bright, broken pieces of glass, and "wax crosses supporting artificial vines." Sarah thought the crafts a "waste of time" and kept her home "free from display but not without comfort." The young Bertha created mischief at her relative's home; she stole supplies to attempt her own craft projects and went to the closet where her aunt's and cousin's shoes were kept, "lacing every pair to the high vamps."

Joshua proclaimed himself an atheist but did not restrict his wife from attending church or having the girls go to prayer meetings, revivals, and Sunday school. After observing a baptismal ritual in the village millpond, he compared the newly converted to his sheep. Just like farm animals, the newly baptized were "doused in the mill pond, then fleeced good in church." While Bertha led prayers at church meetings, she shared her father's skepticism on religious matters. A game of hunting for naughty words in the Bible gave Bertha's parents the impression that she had developed a passion for the Good Book. A school friend had discovered what Bertha described as "good old Anglo-Saxon words" in the book and challenged Bertha to find the most "nasty words." Sarah was especially pleased to see her younger daughter studying the Bible and marking pages with bits of paper

As Joshua found "a note of dishonesty in the myth of Santa Claus," gifts for the girls were never saved until a particular day but were shared as an ordinary treat. The Van Hoosens did not decorate a tree for Christmas, but they made a special meal of oysters and turkey and hung stockings for the girls.

Bertha was aware that her family was more financially comfortable than some of the other farm families. Joshua told his daughters that there was sufficient money for the family but not "one cent for you to futter away." Bertha took it upon herself to create a community giving tree for the other village children. Year round, the creative child fashioned gifts from scraps found in her mother's rag bin: treasures of shells, bits of colored glass and colored stones from the creek bed, feathers, walnut shells, and bits of wood and metal found around the farm. The community tree stood in her father's tool shed and was decorated with strings of cranberries, popcorn, and stars cut from food tins. Alice dressed as Santa, and her mother shared cider and donuts as the neighborhood children filed past Bertha to receive their homemade gifts.

Celebrations on the farm never included alcoholic beverages. Joshua learned early the dangers of drink. An older brother had succumbed to the cold when, heavily intoxicated, he attempted to walk home from Rochester on a bitterly cold New Year's Eve.

The village square was split in two by a dirt lane that led from the Van Hoosen farmhouse to Stoney Creek School District 1, the village's one-room schoolhouse. Both Van Hoosen girls were educated in the ungraded village school. Each day they learned their own lessons and listened to the lessons of the older children. Bertha felt that listening to the older students' work helped improve her own, and by the age of ten, she was more advanced than the children who attended the grade school in nearby Rochester. Men held the teaching position for most of the years that Alice and Bertha attended the village schoolhouse. Discipline was strict and corporal with a leather strap used on farm boys who misbehaved. Girls were not flogged but were hit on the hand with a ruler until "they no longer drew the hand away." Unaccustomed to the use of physical force even on farm animals, Bertha wrote that it made her ill to see the strap used on her classmates.

Rural schools had two terms. The summer term was short; the class was made of girls and younger children, while the older boys helped on the farms. Most children attended the winter term that, by law, had to be at least three months long.

The town of Rochester offered an alternative to the one-room school. Started as a subscription school in 1847, the Rochester Lyceum was one of only twelve graded schools in Oakland County. Parents wanting a better education for their youngsters contributed enough money to buy the site and materials for the school. Built on a hill west of the town's main street, the building had a commanding view of the surrounding area and a grove of trees for the scholars' recreation. By 1865, the Lyceum had become part of the public school system as Rochester District 5. Believing, as it turned out incorrectly, that attending the Lyceum would help his daughters to be accepted to the University of Michigan, Joshua enrolled them.

It wasn't until attending the Lyceum that the Van Hoosen girls noticed the difference between themselves and the townspeople. Bertha realized that her father's boots were greased instead of shined, his hat was outdated, and his homemade trousers were different from those of the men in Rochester. Their buggy was covered with mud, and Joshua used a whittled stick rather than a whip as he carted his daughters into town on the road cut by their Taylor ancestors. The Van Hoosen girls and the other farm children were taunted as hayseeds and rubes, clodhoppers and rustics.

Alice was more affected by the comments, and she struggled to have the family practice better table manners, dress better, and keep the buggy clean. The sensitive young woman ironed from "dawn till dusk" to "remove the wrinkles from wide petticoats, long drawers, tucked and deruffled nightgowns" and her "Father's boiled shirts." Bertha felt herself superior to the town's children, recognizing early that her lifestyle was healthier. The Van Hoosens owned their own home and had better and more abundant food, and she was taken to country fairs and Sunday school picnics. Joshua was an active member of the Grange, a social and educational organization devoted to alleviating rural isolation. His family took part in the organization's many activities while he served as the chairman of the Rochester Grange.

At school, Bertha easily bettered the other children in class work. She enjoyed all the subjects but was especially interested in arithmetic. She frequently lit the kerosene lamp on her bed stand as early as four o'clock in the morning to continue working on a problem that had stumped her the night before. At twelve, she taught older students "intellectual arithmetic" and entered high school at thirteen as a sophomore.

For their secondary work, the sisters had to attend high school in the larger city of Pontiac, which had subscription schools as early as 1822. Its first high school was built in 1846. It was a private school with four terms per year and a tuition of three dollars per term. Situated in an oak grove of nine acres at the intersection of Huron and While Lake Roads, the three-story building had a tower and large lecture hall.

Because the Van Hoosens planned to have their daughters attend college, they needed to enroll them in a school accredited by the state university in Ann Arbor. In 1837, the University of Michigan had established its first preparatory school in Pontiac. The Oakland branch, open to male students only, closed in 1849. The Pontiac high school that Alice and Bertha attended was one of the schools in the state whose pupils were admitted to the University of Michigan without examination on presentation of a proper diploma.

For the Van Hoosen daughters, attending high school meant living away from home for the first time. Due to the differences in his daughters' ages, Joshua made the twelve-mile journey to Pontiac to drop the girls off for their first class on Monday morning and bring them home on Friday afternoon for six years. The scholars left Stoney Creek at five o'clock in the morning and were never late for an eight o'clock class. A brick heated in the farm oven, and used to rest cold feet on, warmed the winter mornings. Lodging was found among the local boarding houses in Pontiac, and the sisters shared quarters with other girls from Avon Township. Under the watchful eyes of the landladies, the girls visited with other students, sometimes annoying the home's proprietors with late-night callers. Bertha reported a landlady who complained about the amount of wood she and her roommates used staying up late to study their lessons.

Holidays were celebrated with simple treats such as molasses candy at Halloween and homemade gifts for Christmas. Entertainment was found at the local churches, and both girls reported to their parents about the lectures and concerts they attended at the Universalist and Unitarian houses of worship. Bertha was eager to mock the congregations she visited. She told her sister that "Old Red Dress" (as she called the Rochester Universalist minister, Miss Wooley) had been "spouting, bashing, shooting off, or whatever you call it." Complaining about the "wretched" singing at a funeral that made her teeth "grit," she wrote that she "wouldn't have an orthodox minister make a prayer over a dog of mine." Baptists received special condemnation for their "barbarous" practice of dipping believers in cold water.

Alice was popular with both sexes. After Alice's graduation, Bertha wrote to relay the greetings of young men and report on the romantic interests of friends. Alice was "worshipped" by one fellow or another, and she made an impression on classmates and teachers alike. She participated in activities in Rochester, and she became the recording secretary of the Rochester Literary Society when it organized in 1872. Her parties and excursions with friends were often highlighted in the local paper, the *Rochester Era*.

Both Alice and Bertha did well in their class work. They happily wrote to their parents about each passing grade and their love of learning. Alice was selected to read an original composition at the yearly junior exhibition; Bertha proudly told her parents that "no girl passed higher" than her, and she had bettered "the boys and all," earning the highest grade in Latin. Because she was unable to enter college until the age of sixteen, Bertha remained in Pontiac for an additional year after completing her required courses at fifteen. She earned college credit by taking additional classes in French, German, Latin, and Greek.

Bertha later wrote that she was proudest of her father's pleasure when she reported her successes on their Friday evening ride home. As an adult, she reported that her greatest sorrow was when she disappointed him by lying to him. She was invited on a Friday night date in Detroit to see the famous actor Edwin Booth in *Hamlet*, but she neglected to tell her father that she would be in a young man's company when she asked for permission to stay an additional night in Pontiac. Wracked by guilt, she could not enjoy the theater and admitted her failing at the dinner table the next night. Joshua said, "I am sorry" as tears rolled down his cheeks.

In July 1880, the *Rochester Era* reported that Bertha graduated from Pontiac High School with honors and a "fair delivery of the salutatory." The article mentioned Alice's graduation from the University of Michigan that same week. Bertha recalled that she always knew she would attend college. From birth she was "congenitally catalogued" for higher learning. The Van Hoosens were not alone in seeking higher education for their children. Many of their neighbors planned to send their daughters and sons to the university, but prior to 1871, their tax dollars supported only education for young men.

By the 1860s, the University of Michigan–Ann Arbor was the largest university in the country and the most prestigious of any college west of New England. Established by a legislative act in 1817, the issue of women's admission was first discussed in the 1850s against a background of the antislavery and suffrage debates. The university regents asked if it would be a mistake to educate women for anything other than their proper "sphere." Others asked if women were intellectually capable and physically rigorous enough for higher education. Quakers joined the debate, emphasizing the value of the individual human being and favoring equal education. Petitioners pressed for women to be admitted.

In 1858, a committee was formed to study the question. Governor Bingham was reported as being in favor of women's admittance, while the faculty was bitterly opposed. By the late 1860s, the state legislature issued a joint resolution, stating that the "high objects for which the University of Michigan was organized will never be fully attained until women are admitted to its rights and privileges." A female seminary was proposed, but in the end, economics forced a decision. Citing that the university's original statute declared that it was to be open to all, families like the Van Hoosens, with only daughters, questioned why their children were unable to attend schools supported by their tax dollars. In the fall of 1868, university president Erastus Otis Haven announced that it was wrong to deny women the use of publicly supported institutions, but it wasn't until 1870 that a resolution passed and women were admitted. Madelon Stockwell was the first woman admitted to the university in 1870. By September 1871, thirty-three women comprised 3 percent of the school's enrollment.

The campus that the first female students found was little more than open country with unpaved paths that were frequently deep in mud. The original nine buildings were undistinguished. In 1871, construction began on University Hall. It would serve as the home of the Literary College where many female scholars followed their academic paths in its lecture rooms, chapel, and auditorium.

Ann Arbor residents greeted the female students with coldness, scorn, and sometimes outright hostility. Boarding houses were coed and difficult to find. Students paid approximately two dollars a week for rent and another two dollars for food (firewood was extra). Plumbing consisted of outdoor privies, which contributed to recurrent epidemics of typhoid fever.

In 1876, Alice Van Hoosen arrived in Ann Arbor with a wardrobe of "tucked, ruffled, and embroidered petticoats, corset covers, drawers, and nightgowns" that she had labored to make with the assistance of a great-aunt. Alice counted pennies and was careful not to waste any of her parents' hard-earned funds. In the Van Hoosen household, the female members earned money from butter or egg sales or gifts, but Joshua had "the pocketbook." Joshua and Sarah had difficulty discussing finances, and the late summer was tense when mother and daughter approached Joshua for money for the next school term. Bertha developed a theory of family finances, which she called "the family purse," while watching her sister and mother grovel for school expenses. She abhorred the control that one person could exert by controlling the finances. When her turn came, Bertha told her mother to let her handle the financial question. She announced that she would need $300 for the entire school year and insisted that she would send her father an account of every cent she spent. Her father agreed and bypassed his wife, sending Bertha money whenever she asked.

TWO

Dear Friend, Sister, Companion, Guide

— ❧ —

*I*n the 1880s, the only acceptable career for an educated young woman was teaching. Both Alice and Bertha began their college careers in the university's literary department.

Alice thrived; she made a positive impression on her professors and was elected to class office. When offered a teaching position before graduation, she declined, hoping to be recommended by an acquaintance at Wellesley College in Massachusetts, but she was told that there was no place for her at the institution, because she was not a "good working Christian." After earning her degree, she worked at a school ten miles north of the farm, "boarding around" with district families. She accepted an invitation to teach in East Saginaw, one of the cities developed on either side of the Saginaw River and financed by a flourishing lumber industry.

Superintendents frequently sought new teachers through inquiries to the university, and Alice was not the first teacher to join the Saginaw staff by way of Ann Arbor. East Saginaw's school superintendent was Joseph Comstock Jones. Born in 1841, Jones had been raised in the Quaker community of Adrian, Michigan, where his father, Eliphalet Jones, had emigrated from Cayuga County, New York. A handsome boy with a deeply dimpled chin, Jones was one of four children born to Eliphalet and his second wife, Lydia Field.

Jones began his education in rural, one-room schools and the Raisin Valley Institute, a secondary school founded by Quakers. As a young man, he changed jobs frequently, taught in Detroit and Tecumseh, ran for political office as a Republican, and considered studying medicine. An 1874 letter from his older half-brother, Professor Elisha Jones, advised the newly married Joseph to "finish your course of study and get into some supporting business as soon as you can." Jones followed his brother to an advanced degree in classical studies at the University of Michigan. He found employment with the Pontiac School District as a superintendent during the Van Hoosen girls' tenure there. He was a popular administrator who was referred to as "JC" by Alice and her friends. In 1877, he joined the East Saginaw School District and relocated with his wife, Nettie, and young son, Edward Horton.

During the peak years of the lumber era, East Saginaw experienced a boom in civic improvements and public education. Alice was employed at the new East Side High School, and Jones had overseen the construction. Two stories tall, the brick building had eleven rooms and seating capacity for 282 students. It was the first Saginaw school with the luxury of central heating.

Alice taught Greek history and elementary exercises in Greek and Latin in a curriculum that included algebra, geometry, bookkeeping, natural philosophy, political economy, and German and English literature. She was one of only two teachers mentioned by name in a school district history of the decade, and her students remembered her as inspiring their love of literature and making ancient Rome and Greece come alive for them. One student remembered the diminutive Alice sitting on her legs to appear larger behind her teacher's desk. The school day was comprised of one session from 8:30 a.m. to 1:30 p.m., but on Fridays, Alice held a special afternoon session for the students who were eager to learn more.

Alice's salary of $650 per year did not support the lifestyle she had dreamed of. She was often lonely, always low on funds, and she frequently asked her parents to loan her money. She confided to Bertha her lonesomeness and the stress of not being able to have the clothing she wanted. Fashion was of great consequence to her. Her letters were full of details of fabric and style, critiques of others' clothing, advice to her mother and Bertha, and a longing for things better than what she had. After receiving a particularly miserable letter from her in 1884, Bertha wrote, "The state of your wardrobe has a great deal to do with your nervous system."

While calling herself an old maid, Alice had a short-lived, unenthusiastic engagement to a gentleman she referred to as Kean.

The correspondence between the sisters became more emotional. Bertha addressed Alice as "Dear friend, sister, companion, guide," and her frequent letters from Ann Arbor were almost romantic in her longing for her older, idealized sister. They wrote of sharing a future when "people will respect us for what we have done." Alice wrote to her "blessed little sweetheart" that one day they would live in a mansion and ride in a closed carriage together. She was "leaving no stone unturned to earn as much money as I can." Additional income meant teaching china painting to earn extra cash and asking Jones for a raise.

Alice found lodging in the large, elegant homes of East Saginaw. In 1883, she boarded with Jones and his family at 134 Maple Street. A friendship developed between the young, single woman and her boss's wife. Nettie enjoyed the gossip and discussion of fashion that frequently filled Alice's letters home. Alice was fond of young Horton and included him on her vacations to the Stoney Creek farm.

Jones was an important and appreciated administrator. During his tenure at East Saginaw High School, it rose in rank among the state's schools and was accepted as a preparatory school by the university. In 1883, he was named as one of the trustees established by the estate of the lumber baron Jesse Hoyt, and he was responsible for administering the donation of four city lots and $100 million for building a public library. In 1885, Jones inaugurated the first free textbook system in the state, which garnered the attention of New York publishing house, Harper Brothers. A job offer followed, and in the spring of 1886, Jones moved his family to New Jersey.

Nettie and Alice continued their friendship through the mail. Nettie told the envious younger woman of excursions into Manhattan to see a production of "The Mikado" by Gilbert and Sullivan and enjoying the famous actor Edwin Booth in *Othello*. Alice returned letters that complained about the new superintendent and a return of her loneliness.

Bertha entered the Literary Department at the University of Michigan in 1880. Her older sister insisted that she wear her long, red hair wound around her head "like a cap." Alice also encouraged Bertha to wear a white muslin apron. Bertha complied even though she saw no other students wearing the accessory. The bright seventeen-year-old soon caught the eye of her Latin professor, Charles Mills Gayley. The handsome Irishman had earned his doctorate at Ann Arbor, and he composed the Michigan college songs, "The Yellow and Blue" and "Laudes atque Carmina." He asked Bertha to remain after a lesson on the love poems of Catullus and inquired if she received gentleman callers. Unprepared for the question, Bertha blurted, "I never did, but I would." She spent many evenings with the professor with the "heart-robbing smile," naively unaware that she was being courted.

On a moonlit night, Gayley faced her and took her hands in his own. Flustered, she pulled away and said she thought he was a "bad man." Explaining that she was alone and far from home, she said, "You are my teacher, and I expect you to treat me as my parents would wish me to be treated." She later wrote that she regretted their "spat." Gayley continued to call during Bertha's sophomore year when she decided to pursue "a social curriculum." He frequently found her busy with tennis, whist, or playing poker with her roommate and male students. Her calendar filled with skating and sledding in winter, twice-weekly dances, and other entertainments, and she found no time for his attention. Gayley soon accepted a position at the University of California–Berkley.

The summer between her sophomore and junior years found Bertha at home on the farm, while Alice remained in East Saginaw. Frustrated and frequently in financial difficulty, Alice's despairing letters to her younger sister continued. She found the job of a teacher restrictive with little hope of advancement for a woman. A college professor told her that the land was flooded with female teachers, and unless women chose other fields, the condition would only get worse.

Bertha had never given much thought as to what she would do with her life. Now at home, she took up a cross-legged posture facing the back of her mother's haircloth sofa. She announced, "I will sit here till my mind is made up about what I am going to do with the rest of my life."

She had become intrigued with what were called "hen medics"—female students in the university's medical department. During her freshman year, she met Mary McLean and Harriet Barringer. Bertha described Barringer as "an eye-catcher in a college town." The sophisticated older woman wore a long, ermine cape and a hat made of peacock feathers.

Bertha later joked that the hat and ermine coat attracted her to the medical profession.

Mary McLean had the greatest influence on Bertha. She was the daughter of a pioneer physician from Washington, Missouri, and she spent two postgraduate years at Vassar College before moving to Ann Arbor. Bertha was impressed with the tall, serious woman's enthusiasm for her subject and found herself drawn to the work.

Bertha could see barriers ahead. There was even greater prejudice against admitting women to the medical department than against admitting them to the university in general. Amanda Sanford of Auburn, New York, the first woman to earn a medical degree at Ann Arbor, suffered verbal abuse at her graduation ceremony. Female medical students were seen as an economic threat, and male physicians were loath to share patients.

While her family laughed at her perch on the sofa, Bertha considered the advantages and disadvantages of a medical career. She measured the opportunity for growth as the science expanded, the challenge of constant study to keep current, the social advantage of being an "indispensable" citizen in the community, and memberships in medical and lay societies that afforded opportunities for interesting friendships. She recognized the monetary rewards, the ability to own her own home, and the attractiveness of having her own buggy and horse to make her rounds. She saw the negatives—the loss of sleep, irregular meals, and exposure to weather and disease—but interpreted these as "living life to its fullest," and she "was not afraid of life." Like her father, she intended to be active and vigorous into old age, and she saw the advantage of a career where she could work as long as she wished or as long as "patients had confidence in her and her health permitted." Her only concern was the effect the decision would have on a marriage. She saw herself as eventually marrying, and while the profession would protect her from dependency should she be widowed, it would possess her time and concentration. She justified her concern by thinking that her practice could be an intermittent one that allowed for intervals of motherhood.

Bertha's announcement that she planned to become a doctor was not well received. Sarah cried each time her daughter's career choice was mentioned, and Joshua confided that he could not furnish funds for an effort that hurt his wife so much. After an unsuccessful attempt to persuade Bertha to become a teacher or remain on the farm, Joshua announced that he would not fund a medical education.

Undeterred, Bertha created her own premed curriculum and supported herself by waiting tables, peddling scales to farmers' wives, and picking berries. Having completed her requirements for an undergraduate degree at the end of the first semester of her senior year, she entered medical school at once, hoping to receive credit for a year in medical school before graduation.

At her first visit to a medical class, she saw the reaction of the male students to their female counterparts. When a female student entered the room, she witnessed the men making "a clucking sound and throwing paper wads and kisses." She decided that she would "elude these men students" by dressing in a manner that she hoped would help her to hide among them. After buying black material, she fashioned a dress "as simple and plain as a nun's habit," and she created a plush bonnet tied with strings under her chin. She decided to keep her intentions secret from her college friends, but she accidently announced her studies when she dropped a medical text in her sorority house. She was relieved that the girls treated her announcement with interest and admiration. She reported, "No one ruffled my feathers by calling [me] hen medic!"

After receiving her Bachelor of Arts degree in June 1884, Bertha received an invitation from Mary McLean, who was in her first year of private practice in St. Louis. A position was available for a calisthenics instructor at the Mary Institute, an all-girl college preparatory school. Bertha could earn her medical school tuition while gaining an introduction to medicine by visiting clinics with McLean. Alice advised her to take the offer. The teaching position would please their parents, and it was better than the menial jobs Bertha had been working.

After joining McLean in September, Bertha experienced firsthand the frustrations that female doctors suffered. The women had difficulty finding a landlord willing to rent rooms for an office and sleeping quarters, and none would allow a sign heralding a female doctor's practice. After signing a contract stating that she would never hang a sign or doorplate with the designation Dr. or MD attached to her name, McLean led Bertha to an office in a neighborhood called Scab Row.

On weekends, Bertha accompanied McLean to the operating amphitheater at City Hospital. Unprepared for the sights and sounds observed from their front-row seats, a faint Bertha was twice led away by McLean before she insisted on staying through a complete procedure. Hoping to test out of some of her first-year courses, Bertha studied anatomy and chemistry. Bertha was frustrated by her inability to memorize a freshman anatomy text, and McLean told her that anatomy had to be learned in the dissecting room, sitting at the side of a cadaver.

McLean was a devout Catholic. In later years, when she had a large practice and was one of the leading surgeons in St. Louis, she began each surgery with a prayer. Bertha mocked McLean's frequent prayers, adherence to dietary restrictions, and refusal to read anything but the Bible on Sundays. Though different in temperament, the women remained close. When McLean was appointed a resident physician at St. Louis Female Hospital, becoming the first woman in St. Louis to serve in a hospital position, she devoted herself to her duties.

Bertha traveled to the hospital twice a week to visit her lonely friend. She observed what her future held as she accompanied McLean on her rounds and saw the doctor spend most of the night writing patient histories and studying difficult cases. Bertha developed a theory of patient-physician relations while observing McLean. Bertha found Mary's bedside manner cold and unsympathetic, and she told her sister that as a doctor she would always be "pleasant and thoughtful, hopeful and sympathetic, and above all things, approachable." She recognized that her childhood on the farm had taught her valuable lessons. She wrote to Alice, "Men and plants are not very different in cultivation. You can't raise pigs from thistles."

The sisters were reunited briefly when the family traveled to the 1885 World Exposition in New Orleans.

As the end of her teaching contract approached, the principal asked Bertha if she would stay another year with an increase in salary. She said, "I intend to study medicine and have too little confidence in myself not to keep my eye on the goal." The principal put his arm around her and told her that he had once wanted to be a lawyer, but marriage and a family had kept him in a safe teaching position. He said, "You are a wise little girl. Keep to your singleness of purpose."

When Bertha departed in August, McLean was still waiting for her first private patient after a year in practice. Bertha wrote that her time with McLean "opened my eyes to the prejudice, the discrimination, the lack of confidence and paucity of opportunities that had to be reckoned with before success could be secured."

Bertha returned to the University of Michigan in 1885. She stood for oral exams and received credit for the first year of medical studies. Having already earned an undergraduate degree and spending a year observing clinics in St. Louis, she started medical school well in advance of her fellow students whose only entrance requirement was a high school diploma.

The University of Michigan was one of the few coeducational medical schools in the United States, and the student population was 25 percent female. Prior to the 1880s, female medical pioneers had founded separate schools staffed and managed by women, but most female medical students preferred acceptance into orthodox medical schools. The women-only schools were frequently seen as inferior even though they offered the advantage of female role models and exposure to women's hospitals and dispensaries.

The medical school was housed in a three-story building on a dirt road on the eastern edge of the campus. Bertha found that she was uncomfortable back in Ann Arbor. While the medical school professors and some male students were accepting of the female medical students, others at the school were not. She wrote to Alice that she kept to herself to avoid the prejudice against hen medics. She continued to dress in simple, black dresses and wrap her red hair around her head in heavy braids. She told her sister that she would never raise her eyes from the ground, and while in class, she would direct her attention solely to the professor.

Bertha's school days coincided with the tenure of the university's president James Burrill Angell, a charismatic and paternal figure. He and his wife did their best to help the female medical students feel at ease, but the harassment continued. Bertha found that she was the recipient of unwanted male attention. When invited to dinners and parties by professors, other students, and even her dentist, Bertha exhibited a determination to avoid anything that would distract her from her purpose. "I have a bulldog grip on the coattail of the medical man," she wrote her sister, "and I shall have his coat or his blood," adding, "I really don't mind anything when my eyes are on the goal."

The subjects for the second-year curriculum included lectures on physiology, *Materia medica* (pharmacology), therapeutics, obstetrics, diseases of women and children, and systematic surgery. She wrote of her admiration for her professor of surgery, Dr. Donald McLean. Unrelated to Mary McLean, he was trained during the Civil War. McLean was a tall, handsome Scotsman who laughed at the new theory of the effect of germs and sterile preparation for surgery. Bertha wrote that the germ theory would have hampered his "dramatic technique." Rolling up the sleeves of his freshly starched shirt, he would drop the knife after making an incision and thrust his ungloved hand deep into the patient. Bertha compared his surgical skill to a bird of prey. He swiftly opened his patients and performed surgery with precision and accuracy. She felt his mortality rate wasn't higher because of his speed.

The future surgeon especially enjoyed her anatomy instructor, Dr. Croydon Ford, and his detailed instruction. His inspiring classes provided the knowledge of the human form that she would need. Bertha was moved to consider that she did not know her lesson "unless I knew everything remotely related to it as well as everything directly connected with it." The female students dissected separately from the men in what had been Ford's office in the medical building. Many cadavers were needed (125 to 140) per year to fulfill the demands of the busy dissecting labs. Occasionally, Bertha found herself in embarrassing situations. She complained to Alice that she had been given a male cadaver for dissection. A female replacement was quickly found. Many medical school classes were coed unless they touched on subjects that were deemed too sensitive for mixed audiences such as urology. Admitting years later that much of the knowledge that she received in medical school had become obsolete, she said that "anatomy remains the same, yesterday, today and forever." The inspiration given by her professors "continued unchanged throughout the years."

Medical school costs included a matriculation fee, tuition, and laboratory and demonstration fees. With her earnings exhausted after her second semester, Bertha applied for the position of a medical-student nurse at the Women's Hospital and Foundling's Home in Detroit. The institution was established in 1868, and its patients were mostly unmarried women about to become mothers. The future obstetrician observed her first human birth and remembered every detail as she wrote her autobiography years later; she described the tiny infant as the "victor in the race with life and death."

Observing childbirth and tending the mothers and babies kept her senses at a fevered pitch. When spending a weekend at the farm near the summer's end, she awoke to find herself trying to empty a startled Alice's breast in her sleep. The next morning, Joshua and Sarah forbade Bertha to return to the job.

Lacking the funds needed to return to school, Bertha accepted an offer to teach in East Saginaw with Alice. The sisters roomed together while Bertha taught German and mathematics.

After leaving East Saginaw for East Orange, New Jersey, in 1886, the Jones family had thrived. Nettie and Horton enjoyed the cultural events of New York while Jones took charge of the schoolbook department of Harper Brothers, working with authors like James Baldwin. He kept a lively correspondence with his youngest sister, Myra, who was an art teacher in Detroit. While Myra extolled a progressive spirit in education, Joseph defended the status quo, telling her, "It is a fine thing to talk of individuality. Successful work comes with teaching one thing well by teaching continuously, drill, drill, drill." Nettie stayed in frequent contact with Alice, discussing fashion and gossip. She advised her young friend on her relationships and career options. Alice considered leaving teaching for pharmacy or medical school. She followed her sister's example and enrolled in the medical school in Ann Arbor. Nettie felt that it was a bad idea and that Alice did not have the "scientific mind" that Bertha did.

Tragedy struck in June 1887 when Nettie and her infant died in childbirth. Devastated and with a young son to care for, Jones continued his work at Harper Brothers and carried on his deceased wife's correspondence with Alice.

Bertha hoped to join Alice in Ann Arbor, so she applied for and won a position as a demonstrator of anatomy at the medical school assisting Dr. Ford. With her BA accepted as credentials and a salary of fifty dollars a month, Bertha spent the summer of 1887 in Ann Arbor to prepare. Rising early and dissecting from four o'clock in the morning until noon each day, Bertha shared her cadavers with a "tall, pale, city-bred fellow who became easily tired and took frequent breaks." Flushed with enthusiasm and the endurance learned on the farm, Bertha spent hours at her task. Colleagues teased her dissecting partner that she was mysteriously taking his strength. They told him that while he got weaker and needed a couch, Bertha grew stronger.

After three months of dissecting and study, Bertha was ready for instruction to begin in October. She was able to fund her education, and she graduated in the spring of 1888. Just before graduation, she was approached to give a donation toward purchasing a dress for another student who had worked her way through medical school. After asking if she would receive a dress because she had also supported herself though school, Bertha was told that she was "different" and would not be given a dress. She remade an old dress as a graduation outfit.

Bertha considered that she was indeed different. "On the farm, I had learned how to meet realities without suffering either mentally or physically...I had freedom to succeed, freedom to fail. Life on the farm produces a kind of toughness."

After graduation, Bertha returned to the Women's Hospital in Detroit to obtain clinical experience.

Alice's commitment to medicine wavered, and along with friends from her teaching days in East Saginaw, she planned a European tour for the summer of 1889. Unknown to her family, the relationship between Jones and Alice had changed. Jones met her in New York to arrange for her passage as well as his own. Alice's plan was to cross the Atlantic with her friends as intended and for Joseph to join her in Europe in September. Writing frequently to her "own dear pet" Bertha, Alice thrilled to the sight of dolphins and flying fish on the ocean crossing. Joking that she had undermined the temperance principles of one of her traveling companions, Alice felt she had escaped sea sickness by drinking beer. She wrote from London of an Englishman who "dropped his *H*s and put them in again in queer places." The British "stepped quietly and spoke softly," and she was charmed. "I have been absolutely happy, and you know how rare that is for me."

Alice wrote to Jones from Paris, instructing him to register in a different hotel than her own so as not to cause either embarrassment. In a letter to Bertha dated September 4, 1889, Alice explained that Jones would be with her in London by the time the letter reached Bertha. She gently told her sister that she was to marry Jones. "Don't think that any love will ever be so great that it can crowd out my darling sister from the place that is hers and hers alone," Alice wrote. She added, "I hope I will have a dear little baby that we both will love."

Alice and Joseph married in the London district of St. Giles on September 13. The groom, described on the wedding license as a widower and publisher's superintendent, was forty-eight years old. The bride, listed only as a spinster, was thirty-four years old, and she wrote her sister to say that the "wedding was not a solemn one but funny. We were married in a dirty old registrar's office. The ceremony was a very simple one, and we said the words ourselves." The newlyweds embarked on a honeymoon trip across the English countryside.

In Michigan, the *Rochester Era* ran an announcement of the wedding. Bertha wrote her sister that the local gossips were having a good time discussing the nuptials. "They thought the reason you were married away from home was because Father disapproved of the match," Bertha wrote. Instead Joshua and Sarah basked in well wishes and looked forward to welcoming their son-in-law to Stoney Creek. Referring to comments about the change in her relationship with her sister, Bertha said, "I'd rather be fifth best and feel that you are happy than be first and feel that I could not make you happy."

Before beginning married life in New Jersey, Alice and Joseph visited family in Stoney Creek and Ann Arbor. Alice met her in-laws for the first time and was uncomfortable with Joseph's mother but fond of his sister, Myra. Her stepson Horton was "one big exclamation point of bliss—ah what a delight."

Bereft of the sister she had planned to share her life with, Bertha momentarily lost confidence in her future as a physician. "Responsibility for the life of a patient frightened me," she later wrote. Internships and residencies were not yet part of a medical education for Bertha and her contemporaries. Male students frequently found work with a preceptor or mentor, but male physicians often refused to take on female medical school students as assistants. While her classmates sought to launch private practices, Bertha created her own residency program and returned to the Women's Hospital and Foundling's Home in Detroit.

Van Hoosen Farm 1877
The History of Oakland County, MI 1877

JOSHUA VANHOOSEN.   MRS. JOSHUA VANHOOSEN.

Bertha Van Hoosen c. 1869   *Alice Van Hoosen c. 1869*

The Van Hoosen Farmhouse

Bertha Van Hoosen c. 1880   *Alice Van Hoosen c. 1872*

Bertha Van Hoosen (bottom center), University of Michigan

The Van Hoosen farmhouse parlor. From left: Joshua Van Hoosen, Bertha Van Hoosen, Alice Van Hoosen Jones, Joseph Comstock Jones, Horton Jones, Sarah Taylor Van Hoosen c. 1891

Sarah Van Hoosen Jones c. 1892   *Bertha Van Hoosen c. 1889*

THREE

Overcoming a Medical Practice Inferiority Complex

—⟨∞∞⟩—

ittle had changed in the Detroit facility since Bertha first labored at the Women's Hospital and Foundling's home in 1886. She arrived to find an epidemic of new mothers suffering from puerperal fever, an infection resulting from the use of contaminated instruments, dressings, and bedding. Familiar with Dr. Joseph Lister and his work on antiseptic techniques, Bertha worked with the nurses to clean the entire hospital by soaking sheets and the gowns of patients and doctors in a toxic bichloride of mercury solution. With no room to segregate newly delivered patients from infected ones, the process was repeated daily. After a month of exhausting work, the epidemic ceased, and Bertha could sleep without the nightmare of losing a patient to sepsis.

Bertha was responsible for conducting all the deliveries, and she prided herself on not having to ask for help from the attending male obstetricians. Later in her employment, a difficult case forced her to ask for assistance in applying forceps, a skill she had seen only in medical books. She felt the answering physician treated her with condescension. He made comments about the procedure needing masculine strength and made her feel "inferior because I was a woman—an irremediable condition."

After serving as resident for six months, Bertha was invited to return to Ann Arbor to teach anatomy during the winter months. She accepted and was pleased to return to the dissecting room where she "felt the presence of the Divine Architect of man more keenly than when I entered a church." She missed Alice, who was living on the East Coast with her husband. "My heart goes out farther and farther every day, and some days

I feel as if it would draw me away clear to New Jersey to see my darling girl," she wrote.

With classes ending in the spring, Bertha again sought a position that would provide clinical experience and a steady income. She heard of an opening at the New England Hospital for Women and Children in Boston. Describing herself as a twenty-six-year-old graduate of the University of Michigan Medical School and offering to send references, she applied for the post but was rejected. An acquaintance who recently left the position of assistant physician at the Kalamazoo State Hospital for the insane inquired if Bertha would be interested in filling the vacancy. What little experience she had with the mentally ill had left her shaken, but the salary of seventy-five dollars per month, along with room and board, helped her to overcome her hesitancy.

In Kalamazoo, Bertha's duties included the gynecological care of 450 insane women and medical charge of some wards. Early female medical school graduates found asylum work appealing, because it allowed them to gain experience treating a variety of ailments and a chance to make contacts that would be helpful later in their career. As the only woman on a staff of eight, Bertha was the frequent target of practical jokes. She was told that it was her duty to extract the teeth of any patient who went to the dispensary on Fridays, and she estimated she extracted a thousand teeth before the superintendent discovered what was happening.

While offering patients safety, a regular routine, and occasional medications, nineteenth-century treatment for the insane was little more than detention. Bertha examined each female patient brought to the asylum and made a record of any marks or bruises found on her body. Having had no instruction in psychiatry at medical school, she came to see insanity as "a living death more than a disease."

She found herself suffering profound loneliness. Her letters to Alice took on a despairing tone, much like Alice's earlier correspondence from East Saginaw. When stricken with typhoid at the end of her contract, Bertha hovered close to death. Beckoned from New Jersey, Alice wrote Joseph that her parents had been summoned, and "we fear the worst for Bertha." After spending a week in a coma and losing all her hair, Bertha recovered.

Eager to leave the asylum and again hearing of an opening at the New England Hospital for Women and Children, Bertha wrote a more convincing application letter. She was invited to Boston for an interview. She stopped in New Jersey so that she and Alice could shop for an appropriate outfit. Bertha dressed in a diagonal-striped wool dress and matching tunic under a cape with long points in front. She felt self-conscious because of her short, curly hair (the result of the recent bout of typhoid), but she was confident in her experience in obstetrics. She won the position of resident physician at the women's hospital.

The New England Hospital for Women and Children was founded in 1862 by Dr. Marie Zakrzewska, a protégé of America's first female doctor, Elizabeth Blackwell. Bertha described Zakrzewska as homely and old fashioned but possessing a "blaze of power and strength." She believed that she could have been friends with "Dr. Zak" if the woman had not frightened her at their first meeting. Bertha said, "Sitting by my side on a bench in the hospital entrance, she said, intending to encourage me, 'You are getting along splendidly, but you smile too much.'"

The facility Zakrzewska founded was the second hospital in the country to be run by female physicians and surgeons. It opened doors for women who were excluded from clinical opportunities at male-run hospitals.

In her autobiography *Petticoat Surgeon,* Bertha listed her duties as "seeing every patient in the hospital at least once a day, doing one-third of the surgical operations and assisting in the others, conducting all abnormal deliveries, keeping a day book, attending the private clinic twice a week, and last but not least, being responsible for the teaching and deportment of six interns." With her exhausting schedule, she frequently studied through the night, mentally performing unfamiliar procedures in preparation for the morning's surgery.

The opportunity to do surgery fit Bertha's career plan. She was devoted to the practice of obstetrics and understood the antipathy toward women in the field. An early prejudice equated female physicians with abortionists. By the end of the nineteenth century, a female doctor with a specialty in obstetrics was frequently branded a "midwife," a stepchild in the discipline without professional recognition. Bertha believed that there were countless women in society who suffered from gynecological ailments but were too embarrassed to seek aid from a male doctor. She felt that she could help women more as a surgeon and, with her background in anatomy, "enter obstetrics through a surgical door."

Now in closer proximity, the sisters were able to see each other more often. Alice's letters to her mother in Stoney Creek reported of Bertha's visits to New Jersey and Alice's excursions to Boston.

Joseph learned that Harper Brothers planned to cease publishing schoolbooks, and he turned to colleagues in Ann Arbor for letters of recommendation and job leads. His search brought him back to East Saginaw where he was considered for the position of secretary of the Saginaw Improvement Company. Writing to "my darling girls," Jones told his wife and sister-in-law not to "worry more than you can help." To his "darling Alice," he wrote that she needed the "willpower to believe the bright side will come to find cheer where gloom and irritation are." He wished he could hold her "to help you in your trouble." In December 1890, he accepted an opportunity to serve out the school year as superintendent for the school district of Newton, Massachusetts. Alice complained of being unhappy and uncomfortable living in a boarding house in Newton, but her sister was nearby. Alice was able to come to Bertha's side when she fell ill in Boston.

Exhausted and frustrated by the work demands of the resident position, Bertha resigned from the Boston hospital and explained her reasons in a lengthy letter to the board. She complained of "having responsibility over all things but control over none." She felt that patient care suffered as a result of the overburdening of the resident. She explained the frustrations of the interns she worked with and their lack of clinical opportunities due to outdated rules and regulations. She wrote that the hospital management was not under pressure to change, because female physicians did not have enough internship opportunities to choose from. Bertha later wrote that she had become hypercritical of the staff physicians and overly confident.

Needing a rest and learning that her sister was pregnant, Bertha decided to join Alice and Joseph, who were staying in Stoney Creek with her parents. Bertha enthusiastically threw herself into preparation for the baby. The new arrival would have handmade diapers, embroidered blankets, bibs, and dresses. She was most proud of her design for a "papoose pillow," a portable featherbed that secured the infant but left her head and arms exposed. Alice's pregnancy went smoothly, and the family rejoiced at the time they had together. Joshua enjoyed discussing politics with his son-in-law as Bertha and Alice gardened with their mother.

Bertha felt that her years of hospital experience had trained her for what she considered her most important delivery. Alice was thirty-seven, considerably older than most first-time mothers of the era. Jones was fifty and had lost his first child, his third child, and his wife in childbirth. Bertha thought he looked older than his years when Alice announced that the labor pains had begun. Labor dragged into a second day. When the infant's heart stopped beating, Bertha sprang to action and delivered the baby girl by forceps. Finding the child unresponsive, Bertha breathed into her tiny lungs for forty-five minutes. She wrote later that having breathed life into the child, she felt she was as much a parent to her as Alice and Joseph. She wrapped the baby, named Sarah after her grandmother, in her papoose pillow and found a new vision for her future.

While Jones sought employment in the Michigan school districts, Bertha considered a location for her private practice. If she remained in Michigan, her father would help financially—a gift she did not want to accept. Mary McLean offered to share her active St. Louis practice, and a cousin in Milwaukee, the surgeon Ernest Copeland, invited her to work in Wisconsin. An aunt offered an opportunity to visit Milwaukee as part of a Chicago shopping excursion.

Bertha was unimpressed with Copeland's expensively decorated office and unhappy with the predominance of German culture in the Wisconsin city, but she thrilled at her introduction to Chicago. She wrote home to Stoney Creek, "I have been here for two hours and am already in love with the city."

Chicago was in its opulent age. Its location at the center of the nation made it the hub of a vast railway network. Chicago businesses were able to import commodities and export products, generating an explosion in manufacturing and commerce. Elaborately decorated "temple" skyscrapers reached for the heavens, and museums, parks, and exposition centers offered entertainment and relaxation. Cable cars and an elevated railway system facilitated workers, visitors, and shoppers as they traversed the busy streets. The White City, the glimmering site of the 1893 Columbia World's Fair, was under construction along Lake Michigan's shore.

The city did have a dirtier, darker side. Factories belched smoke and cinders, unpaved roads became mud rivers in bad weather, and in poorer neighborhoods, garbage overflowed from collection boxes. Factories attracted immigrants who huddled in the city's slums.

With limited funds and knowing no one in Chicago, Bertha rented a hall bedroom in a house on Congress Street. Her office-bedroom had a couch that she slept on, a Morris chair that could be converted into an examining table, and a bookcase. She paid thirty dollars per month for room and board and had savings enough for ten months.

She needed to have three recognized physicians sign an application for a state license to practice. She had read about surgeon Rachel Hickey Carr, the second woman to intern at Cook County Hospital. When she visited the older woman's office, she found a sympathetic ally. Carr helped her to get signatures from two other physicians: Marie Mergler, a prominent Chicago abdominal surgeon and gynecologist, and Sarah Hackett Stevenson, the first woman admitted to the American Medical Association (AMA).

With her license in hand and an oversized sign filling the window of her third-floor room, Bertha waited for her first patient. Within a week, the druggist who had agreed to take calls for her sent a message that she was to "come at once" to an apartment at Thirty-Sixth and Cottage Grove Avenue. It was the home of Dr. Carr. After admitting that she couldn't resist giving the young woman the thrill of her first medical call, Carr explained that she had been appointed to serve as an emergency physician at the dedication of the Columbian World's Fair. She was now pregnant, and the duty would conflict with the upcoming birth, so Carr wanted Bertha to be her substitute.

Bertha was unaware of the battle that had been waged between Chicago's medical women and the organizers of the fair. When Dr. Stevenson learned that female physicians would have no part in the fair, she got appropriation for a Woman's Hospital Hall. Female doctors gave first aid and treated thousands of patients during the fair. Bertha served at the dedication ceremonies in October 1892 and saw patients in an emergency substation housed in the manufacturing building. With a salary of ten dollars per day and a mention in the press coverage of the World's Fair debut, Bertha's practice received the boost she badly needed.

Her first private patient arrived in the form of an immigrant family's infant who suffered from an acute intestinal infection. Bertha instructed the mother to withhold nourishment for twenty-four hours and give the child frequent enemas, and she mentioned her diagnosis and treatment to a young male doctor at the boarding house. The doctor laughed at her inexperience. He told her that she must always prescribe pills, if only sugar pills, because the illiterate immigrants appreciated only doctors who gave medications. Discouraged that she was expected to "bamboozle" her patients, Bertha returned to check on the infant. She found that the child had improved. The ecstatic mother smothered Bertha in kisses and told anyone who would listen about the lady doctor who had cured her baby. The woman's family and neighbors became Bertha's first clientele.

Bertha's letters to Stoney Creek intrigued Jones. He had yet to find a new position. Chicago was experiencing a real estate boom, and his sister-in-law's description of the growing city inspired him to change careers and take up real estate speculation. He joined Bertha at her boarding house in October 1892. After acquiring heavy mortgages, he bought two houses and vacant land on Calumet.

Alice was left behind in Michigan, and she sank into melancholy reminiscent of her teaching days in East Saginaw. Writing in her diary, she fretted about the baby's health, worrying that if the infant slept too long she might have "brain disease" and fearing that her diary's pages would be "blistered with tears." Bertha patiently answered her sister's concerns in frequent letters to Michigan, advising her on proper formula choices and the local doctor's abilities.

Alice worried about Joseph, and begged him to "not sleep in one of the vacant houses to save a few dollars." She joined her husband in early 1893, and her worries changed to financial issues as the real estate market grew cold and money was an overriding concern. Bertha joined her sister's family in their move to one of the mortgaged houses and created a medical office in the home's lower level.

Bertha needed to fill her time while waiting for patients and wanted to stay "abreast and alive, and nothing will do it so well as being in some work." She applied for the unpaid position of anatomy instructor at Northwestern University Women's Medical School. The institution opened in 1870 as the Woman's Hospital Medical College. It became part of Northwestern University in 1891 and had twenty-four professorships. Bertha devoted every afternoon to dissecting and developed a following of young women who asked to study privately as paying students over the summer. When the students requested credit for the summer course, they were denied and told that the course would have to be taught by the department head's nephew (with the fee being paid to him). Bertha received a notice that her services were no longer needed.

Bertha was eager to stay connected to the University Women's Medical School, so she sought out the professor of obstetrics, Sarah Stevenson, one of the doctors who signed her license application. Stevenson needed an instructor in embryology. Bertha had never studied the subject but, determined to earn the position, she threw herself into preparation. She met with Dr. Frank Wynekoop, professor of embryology at Chicago's College of Physicians and Surgeons, for instruction and incubation of the eggs needed for class demonstration.

Bertha felt that she lacked clinical experience, and she discovered that a dispensary clinic run by Dr. Byron Robinson offered an opportunity to work independently and learn from an experienced physician while sustaining her private practice. Robinson was a Wisconsin native and graduate of the University of Wisconsin who became a highly respected gynecologist and surgeon. His Columbia Clinic was located in the heart of a ghetto. The clinic hours were 8:00 a.m. to 10:00 a.m. each morning, and Bertha was able to schedule private practice patients for the remainder of the day.

Bertha started her practice when regulations regarding the establishment of clinics and hospitals were negligible. After a patient had died in the hospital attached to the Columbia Clinic, both the clinic and the hospital were shuttered. Robinson opened a second clinic and hospital, the Charity Clinic, at Twenty-Fourth and Dearborn Streets. Bertha was offered the gynecological clinic and the chance to operate on every third patient referred from the clinic to the hospital. She saw the opportunity to realize her plan of becoming an independent surgeon.

Early in her second year of practice, Bertha experienced the death of a patient for the first time. While operating with a male colleague, she removed the cystic ovaries of a gynecological patient. Infection began on the second postoperative day, and Bertha remained with the woman for six agonizing days before she died. Self-doubt hounded the young doctor. Should she have left the ovaries intact? Could they have been treated medically? Had she not prepared the patient properly? The patient's death gave her a sense of failure that haunted her for months.

Joshua and Sarah Van Hoosen had reconciled with their youngest daughter's career choice. The family remained close and supportive even though three hundred miles now separated the daughters from their parents. In response to Alice's downhearted letters, Sarah wrote that Joshua suggested that Alice, Joseph, and little Sarah move back to the farm: "There is plenty on the farm for us all, and we are never so happy as when you are all here." Sarah had visited her daughters and toured the Columbia Exhibit while Joshua remained in Stoney Creek to work the farm.

Now sixty-four, Joshua was still an imposing figure. Known locally as the "jolly mayor of Stoney Creek Village," he was a respected, vigorous citizen whose activities were reported in the *Rochester Era*. He was active in the Rochester Grange, county and state fair committees, and the Republican Party. He was instrumental in ensuring that a spur of the Michigan Central Railroad came through the neighboring town of Rochester. To celebrate the birth of his only granddaughter, he planted a grove of maple trees below the Van Hoosen home.

Joshua continued to question traditional religious beliefs. He and Sarah became fans of the orator Robert Ingersoll, the attorney general of Illinois. He was best known for his long speeches on agnosticism and the sanctity of the family. His orations advocating free thought and humanism often poked fun at religious belief. The Van Hoosens traveled to Detroit and paid the giant sum of one dollar to listen to Ingersoll's three-hour talks.

Bertha rushed back to Stoney Creek in June 1894 when she learned that Joshua was ill. He had suffered from a severe headache for several days, and his wife reported that his "gait was peculiar." The normally energetic farmer spent his days in bed. Bertha took him to Detroit by train and had him admitted to Harper Hospital. Unable to determine a cause for his symptoms, Bertha remained at her father's side as he lapsed into a two week long coma and died.

Devastated, Bertha prepared her father's body for burial in Stoney Creek. He had been a stern but loving father. The life he provided had made her the independent woman she was. She wrote later that "hunger for his approval nagged me year after year." Alice lamented in her diary that her "grief that Sarah can never know this noble man" was "unbounded."

Joshua died intestate. According to Michigan's probate law, the estate was to be divided equally between the widow and children. Bertha and Alice petitioned the court to allow their mother to inherit the farm intact. It was decided that Sarah would spend winters in Chicago and summers on the farm in Stoney Creek. Bertha left Alice to arrange for their mother's move to join the family in Chicago and find renters for the family lands.

FOUR

The Essence of Being a Father

———∞———

Bertha returned to a private practice that, according to Alice, was "booming." Her practice concentrated on obstetrics and the general medical care of women and children. Her clientele was still drawn from the immigrant ghettos, and patients visited her in the lower flat of Alice and Joseph's home on East Forty-Second Street on Chicago's south side.

The family referred to the house as an "English basement house." It had high ceilings and long stairways. Sarah Jones remembered straining to return to her parent's upper floors from Bertha's lower office flat as a small child. The flat contained a waiting room, an examining room that also served as the doctor's bedroom, and a laboratory in what would have been the kitchen.

Bertha struggled with the financial side of her career. She was never sure of what to charge for a service and felt awkward bringing the matter up to her patients. She reasoned that her patients fell into three types: those who always paid their bill, those who never paid a bill, and those who paid as much as was humanly possible. "Every day, I plucked up enough cash laid on my desk so that I never had to draw on the three hundred dollars I had saved to start my career. Often I was able to add to it."

She enjoyed sojourning in the city. She enjoyed the unusual street names, the many parks, and the architecture. She rode cable street cars and climbed the long steps to the "elevated" (the "L"), Chicago's recently inaugurated electric traction train. She later wrote in her autobiography that when she rode the elevated, she "experienced the thrill that an airplane gives youngsters today." She frequently traveled into dangerous neighborhoods, leaving her home at any hour that a patient needed her. She rode the "L" "as far as Roosevelt Road" and then walked over a mile

41

along a viaduct spanning innumerable railroads. She was told that men would not cross that viaduct at night "for fear of thugs." Bertha reported that "although it was weird and lonely, I never met anyone."

She did report suffering a "terrible fright" soon after starting her practice when she was woken at four o'clock on a Sunday morning. A sixteen-year-old boy in a "ramshackle" buggy asked her to accompany him to a home where a baby was having convulsions. Suspicious of the young man, Bertha recalled the case of the murder of Dr. Patrick Cronin. Cronin had accompanied a man in a buggy in the middle of the night and was found murdered two weeks later. Cronin was an active member of an Irish American organization but had become a whistle blower, and his murder was meant to silence him. The lurid stories of his violent death remained in the public consciousness.

Bertha answered her early morning summons. She found an infant suffering a high fever and was able to convince the child's skeptical father to let her lower the burning baby into a tub of cold water.

As her practice grew, she rented transportation for her numerous forays to patients' homes and finally purchased a horse and buggy for seventy-five dollars. When a German patient offered her a mongrel dog named Fritz, Bertha gained a faithful companion on her rounds. Fritz and the horse, Kit, became familiar sights as they waited for the doctor to emerge from a patient's home. Occasionally the horse would tire of waiting and wander back to Forty-Second Street with the dog tagging along.

To supplement her income, Bertha began a fifteen-year relationship with the Armour and Lewis Institutes. Started by nineteenth-century philanthropists P. D. Armour Sr. and Allen Cleveland Lewis, the institutes offered courses not offered in Chicago's public school system. Bertha taught home economics and first aid.

After accounting for expenses, Bertha gave the remainder of her income to her brother-in-law, Joseph. On his insistence, she opened a savings account and deposited her money. Joseph was still invested in Chicago's real estate market. After the demand caused by the World's Fair abated, real estate went flat. Jones was able to sell the vacant land he had purchased, but the two mortgaged homes remained a problem. Joseph and Alice struggled financially, and he took a loan from Bertha for one building project. To the family's great relief, Joseph was offered a position with the Werner Book Company in May 1894. Werner, the nation's largest publisher of educational books, was headquartered in Chicago, and Joseph was employed as the department's head.

His work enabled Alice to enjoy the life of intellectual stimulation she craved. She corresponded with James Baldwin, one of the most prolific writers of schoolbooks in the nineteenth century, discussing philosophy and his latest fiction. Alice and Joseph enjoyed attending shows and going to dinner at the Palmer House, a luxurious hotel in the city's theater district.

Work and family obligations sometimes separated the couple, and their frequent letters were affectionate. He was Alice's "own darling Joe," and she sent "whole worlds of love to you my dear." In 1896, Alice wrote, "My own darling, this is a perfect day—just as perfect as it can be with almost a thousand miles between us."

Joseph had a difficult time settling into his new position and continued to seek other jobs. He refused an offer to teach at a college in Idaho and asked his son if he would like to live on the East Coast again.

During his high school years, Horton frequently was left in Chicago with Bertha while Joseph traveled on business and Alice and young Sarah spent time in Stoney Creek. The teenager wrote long letters to his stepmother, sharing his interest in the arts and literature and sending playful messages to his little sister. After entering the University of Michigan to study mine engineering, Horton split his time between Ann Arbor, Stoney Creek, and Chicago.

Joseph had rigid ideas for raising his daughter. He instructed that she was to have no religious instruction, explaining that he thought early religious training was "productive of irreverence." He looked eagerly to the time when she would be "a sweet schoolgirl—carrying such pretty books to school and coming home to tell Mama how much she knows."

Bertha's mother, Sarah Taylor Van Hoosen, traveled between Chicago and Stoney Creek and was never completely comfortable in the big city. Bertha tried to entice her with descriptions of the merchandise in the downtown stores, but the recent widow was more comfortable in her familiar surroundings in Michigan. The women found the summer weather in Chicago uncomfortable, and Alice and little Sarah frequently left Joseph, Horton, and Bertha behind to find relief from the humidity among the trees and brooks of the family farm. Alice assumed responsibility for management of the farm's land, now worked by tenants.

Still determined to enter obstetrics "through a surgical door," Bertha continued her internship with Dr. Robinson. Her mentor sometimes "criticized to the point of abuse," but Bertha told visiting doctors, "When I have learned to use the knife, the wounds to my pride and sensibilities will soon heal." She offended Robertson by using another physician's surgical technique that he had denounced. Robinson demanded loyalty to his techniques and stormed out of the operating room when he discovered Bertha's stylistic change. After begging his forgiveness, Bertha agreed to discuss every operation with him before proceeding. She realized that if she was to operate independently, she had to be willing to take the credit or blame for her choices.

After two years of Robinson's tutelage, Bertha felt ready to become an independent surgeon. She later recalled that her first "worthwhile position" was a gynecological service on the staff of Wesley Hospital. One of her early patients needed a procedure she was well prepared for. Nevertheless, within a few postoperative days, the woman was terribly infected, taking weeks to heal. When she was well enough to be taken home from hospital, her husband balked at the large bill. After being told that he must pay the hospital before removing his wife, Bertha reported he told the superintendent, "Very well. You keep my wife." Bertha did not charge a fee for her service, and the man took his wife home.

Bertha discovered that the hospital's nurses were not versed in sterilization. Rather than have a repeat of her patient's infection, she did all her own sterilizing in her home laboratory. She left instructions that for her surgeries, the operating room should be cleaned but have no other preparation. After sterilizing the gowns, sheets, sponges, and other equipment and packing them at home, Bertha arrived early, wiped all the furniture with Lysol, and set up the room. Instead of a nurse, her Chicago mentor, Dr. Carr, assisted in the procedures. There were no more cases of postoperative infection.

Her "delightful hospital service" ended two years later when the hospital closed for the construction of a new building. Unable to get privileges in any of the male-dominated hospitals in the city, she began her affiliation with the Chicago Hospital for Women and Children. It was founded in 1865 by America's first female surgeon, Dr. Mary Harris Thompson, and its original mission was to care for the poor and train nurses. Renamed the Mary Thompson Hospital after its founder's death in 1895, it was the only place a female doctor could get unrestricted privileges.

In 1896, Bertha became the head of the hospital's obstetrical department, increasing her reputation as a surgeon and administrator. Her work on ridding the patients of post delivery fever and repairing severe laceration of the perineum gave her a great deal of pride. Many of the patients turned over to her paid very well, and she found working with other successful female physicians inspiring. She later wrote, "There is no way to estimate the stimulation that a woman derives from her acquaintance with women who have achieved success." She continued her friendship with Mary McLean in Missouri and her association with Drs. Rachael Hickey Carr, Marie Mergler, and Sarah Hackett Stevenson, the physicians who had signed her license application. Chicago was a hub for medical women who challenged the status quo. Bertha met Dr. Rachelle Yarros during her internship in Boston, and now the pioneering social hygienist was practicing in Chicago and working with the Hull Settlement House. She rubbed shoulders with suffragette and obstetrician gynecologist Anna Ellsworth Blount and reformers Drs. Harriet Barringer Alexander and Caroline Hedger.

When she heard that the position of head of gynecology and obstetrics at the University of Michigan Medical School was vacant, Bertha took a night train to Ann Arbor. Dr. Victor Vaughn, her friend and the medical school dean, welcomed her and listened as she expressed her desire for the position. Bertha reported that Vaughn "sadly confessed, you cannot have the appointment, much as I would like to see you get it, because you are a woman." Before parting, Bertha told the dean that she felt a woman must occupy the position of professor of gynecology in a coeducational medical institution.

Bertha heard that the Chicago Hospital for Women and Children planned to set up a school of midwifery and resigned. With the aid of Dr. Carr, Bertha became a member of the staff of Provident Hospital, a training school for African American nurses. She found the service better than that in many larger institutions and frequently sent her own patients there. She especially enjoyed arriving at the hospital early and listening to the trainees sing in an "inspiring Episcopalian service." She continued in the post of attending gynecologist until 1929.

During this time, Bertha came under the influence of Edward Bellamy's 1888 utopian novel *Looking Backward*. The book was a response to the injustices Bellamy saw in the economic and social systems in the second half of the nineteenth century. The fantasy of a worker's paradise foreshadowed the communist movements of the twentieth century: government ownership of all means of production and the citizens' duty to labor in an industrial army. Horton Jones took part in Chicago's Bellamy Club, a student group that met to discuss and propagate the book's ideas, and Bertha was attracted to Bellamy's vision of equality for women. His theory of women as the wardens of humanity's future matched her premise that the choice of a mate was a woman's greatest responsibility. She later wrote that she believed a woman should be the instigator of courtship, because she was best suited to choose the finest father for her future children.

With her private practice taking her into the homes of the poor and uneducated, Bertha experienced firsthand what she called the "sexual slavery" of women. Worse than the bedbugs and lice that she frequently brought home to her own family were the images of women brutalized by their husbands and the physical damage suffered after years of frequent childbearing. She compared her childhood to that of the waifs she encountered on her rounds and gently asked her elderly mother how it was that she and Joshua had only two children, spaced eight years apart. Without sharing any uncomfortable details, Sarah Taylor Van Hoosen explained that Joshua had felt that the couple should have no more children than they could adequately educate. Bertha was grateful for being a "spaced child." She sought to educate young women on the physiology of sex so that they would know how to control the number of their offspring.

Bertha's other interest in educating her patients in scientific methods of child development and sanitation led to her involvement in the Chicago Women's Club. Dominated by well-to-do white women, the Chicago club was among the most active of the nation's many clubs founded in the second half of the nineteenth century. Originally focused on self-improvement, by the 1890s, the club's members sought to improve the plight of immigrant and poor women and children. It welcomed female doctors and offered support and acceptance. The doctors gave the clubwomen the professional expertise and guidance needed to forward the club's women and children's health-care agendas. Bertha took an active leadership role, volunteered her knowledge and time, wrote papers, and gave talks.

Joseph Jones became ill in the spring of 1897. His last portraits show facial puffiness due to his worsening kidney disease, historically referred to as Bright's disease. Alice wrote in her diary that his last days were "a horror to recall." His symptoms of back pain, vomiting, and fever were made worse by a streptococcus bacterial infection of the skin known as erysipelas or Holy Fire. For weeks, he was treated with warm baths, diuretics, and laxatives. Joseph lost his battle in April, leaving Alice a forty-two-year-old widow without income and responsible for her five-year-old daughter and college-age stepson. Jones's estate amounted to the $8,000 mortgage on two houses, a small insurance policy, and an outstanding loan he had made to one of his brothers. Like Michigan, Illinois laws gave two-thirds of the estate to Jones's children. Alice learned that the insurance policy was taken not to protect herself and her young child but to pay for Horton's education. A civil court battle ensued; Alice tried to change the policy's beneficiary and recoup ownership of a house that was given to Horton by the court. The legal action caused a rift between the stepmother and son that continued for the rest of Alice's life.

Bertha took her new role as head of the family seriously. She took out a $10,000 life insurance policy and arranged to take over the mortgage on the home the family lived in. She wrote that she considered financial support "the essence of being a father." When proudly entering the bank the first time a payment was due, Bertha and Alice found themselves rejected by the loan officer who would not accept payment from the women. A lawyer had to be retained, adding to Bertha's frustration at the unfairness of the treatment of women. The insult was compounded when, years later, Bertha sought to make a final payment on the loan only to be told the balance must be paid in gold. This time her lawyer was unable to assist, and she had to return to the bank laden with thousands of dollars in gold coin before the loan could be discharged.

The sisters opened a joint bank account. Although the balance was created by Bertha's income, the funds were considered communal. Alice took over the financial side of Bertha's medical practice, investing the funds in what Bertha would describe as "safe and sound" securities. Alice managed the sisters' home, freeing Bertha to concentrate on her career. Her day was filled with an expanding private practice, multiple teaching positions, affiliations with other female physicians, and a continuing education in surgery and medical developments. Bertha became dependent on Alice as a male physician might be on a wife.

Bertha was an attractive woman who still elicited interest from the opposite sex, but she never responded. She focused on her career and family. Like the other women in the Van Hoosen family, Bertha was "short and plump" according to Sarah Van Hoosen Jones. Her face was rounder than Alice's and framed in thick, red hair that she wore braided and wrapped around her head; it hung below her waist when loose. She enjoyed feminine clothing and often designed her own dresses. Her eyes were blue and steeled with determination. Her closest companion was her sister.

Alice's hair had begun to whiten in her forties, and she soon looked older than her years. Alice was interested in current events and culture, and she was occasionally able to convince Bertha to take an evening off to see a play or concert, but she complained that Bertha was frequently distracted. Bertha later wrote that at the start of her career, she took no vacations, never read newspapers, limited reading to medicine, and seldom allowed her thoughts to wander far from professional duties. At times Bertha was so deep in thought she passed her elevated station several times.

The sisters were separated when young Sarah became ill in 1899. After a day at the beach she developed an insatiable thirst. Bertha took the child on her rounds to keep a close eye on her. Alice displayed the era's bias against female doctors when she complained to her sister that she longed for a mature male doctor who could help her daughter. Bertha understood the lack of confidence people felt for women doctors. "Why would you [trust a woman doctor]?" she wrote. "Woman is reared to put her trust in the male sex. Papa is the head of the house...her husband becomes her lord. Her minister, her doctor, her lawyer, her chauffer, yes, even her milkman is of the opposite sex. I suppose it would be unnatural for a woman to trust a woman doctor."

Sarah was diagnosed with malaria and diabetes insipidus, and Alice was advised to move her to the more moderate climate of Santa Barbara, California, until the child's blood showed no sign of disease. Alice and Bertha wrote frequent letters, often full of longing for each other. Writing from Chicago in 1899, Bertha sounded more like a love-sick suitor than a sister: "I long so for this period of separation to be over," she wrote Alice, "I hope your brave little soul and body will not give out under the strain." Alice became depressed and overprotective of Sarah, moving from one rented home to another if neighbors became too friendly and called on the couple. Sarah and Alice spent time in Pasadena, Coronado, Santa Barbara, Santa Monica, and Sarah's favorite, La Jolla. La Jolla reminded her of her "beloved Stoney Creek...small, comfortable, rural, and friendly."

Bertha visited when her full schedule allowed. Sarah later reported that on one memorable visit, Bertha built her a dollhouse from four empty orange crates. The house was decorated with scraps of wallpaper and images from greeting cards.

After her family's return to Chicago, Bertha contracted spinal meningitis. Her six-month convalescence did not curtail her career. As soon as she was able, she returned to a schedule that included the charge of the obstetrics department at the Mary Thompson Hospital. Her unpaid teaching appointments were demonstrating anatomy and later serving as professor of embryology and gynecology at Northwestern University Women's Medical College. She was disheartened when, without warning, Northwestern closed the Women's Medical School.

As an independent surgeon, Bertha developed a reputation as an excellent operator, specializing in gynecological abnormalities and obstetric complications. Her reputation helped the dean of the College of Physicians and Surgeons, William E. Quine, overcome significant faculty opposition when, in 1902, he invited her to join the faculty as professor of clinical gynecology. Bertha wrote that teaching stimulated the mental growth of the teacher more than the student. She felt that the instructor was placed with a group of educators whose function it was to promote and raise the standards of medical education.

It was in the academic sphere at the College of Physicians and Surgeons that Bertha experienced some of the most strident sexual discrimination of her career. When she worried that her first weekly surgical clinic, a summer term elective, would not be well attended, she determined to present a rare surgical case. She was reminded of a young woman with exstrophy-epispadias complex, a congenital abnormality in which part of the bladder is present outside the body. Bertha paid the patient's way to Chicago and had her admitted to West Side Hospital adjoining the college. She planned to display the patient's condition during the first clinic and operate during the second, but she found the amphitheater empty. Only the two male students who were to assist accompanied her. Angered that she was not given a chance to conduct her clinic, Bertha uncovered the anesthetized woman and shocked the young men with the unusual condition. One young man ran from the room and returned, announcing that the amphitheater was full. Resentment against the female instructor continued with a rebellion against her clinic's final examination and the dean's resulting threat of expulsion.

Gradually, the students began to appreciate Bertha's efforts, and attendance grew. While she never again lacked an audience, her troubles were far from over. The management of West Side Hospital, where clinic patients were admitted, never fully accepted having her patients in their institution and looked for an opportunity to refuse to care for them. Unfortunately, Bertha herself gave them that chance. After a patient's postoperative death, she performed an unauthorized autopsy in the woman's hospital room. Finding the doors of the hospital locked against her and her patients, Bertha improvised a private hospital in a retail building across the street from the College of Physicians and Surgeons clinic. She called her infirmary the "Gynoecium, the name the ancients gave to that part of the building occupied by the women among the better classes."

After acquiring a hospital license, Bertha fitted the ward with six black iron beds and "other furniture of mission type." The storefront window was hung with green denim curtains. The new arrangements made it necessary to transport the surgical subjects across a busy street in any weather before riding an elevator to the college amphitheater.

To alleviate the stress to her patients, Bertha began to use scopolamine-morphine anesthesia, a narcotic and amnesiac. The new pharmaceutical came from Europe and was not yet accepted for general use in the United States. Bertha found opposition to its use in her operations on private patients at the Woman's Hospital and the Frances Willard Hospital. Nurses refused to administer the injections or were told not to carry out the doctor's orders. Bertha's choice of anesthesia was criticized by the lay members of the board of trustees of the hospitals. Overcoming opposition, she had used scopolamine in two thousand surgical cases by 1908.

FIVE

The Elf from the Black Forest

⸺⸰⸰⸺

he dawn of the new century found Bertha's reputation as a physician and surgeon growing. Her numerous teaching positions and surgical clinics introduced her to the next generation of physicians. Her patients were no longer drawn exclusively from Chicago's immigrant ghettos, although she donated valuable time at charity clinics.

Middle- and upper-class patients visited her at her new office in the Reliance Building at 32 North State Street. The fifteen-floor skyscraper was the first to have large plate-glass windows make up the majority of its surface area. Clients were met by a glamorous lobby with extensive iron grillwork and marble floors.

Women of means who were unable to have successful pregnancies sought Bertha. After one woman suffered the deaths of five infants during difficult deliveries, Bertha agreed to perform a cesarean section, which was considered a dangerous operation. In an amphitheater filled with gynecologists, university professors, and surgeons, Bertha delivered a healthy child to the cheers of the six hundred physicians.

When wealthier patients did not send a vehicle to bring Bertha to their homes, she drove an electric car to make her rounds. Though the sisters were separated for months at a time due to young Sarah's illness, Bertha could write to Alice, "I have money now, and you shall have things out there as they should be."

Starting in 1900, Bertha sought to improve and expand her surgical skills by leaving her practice and teaching positions for a week every three months to observe at the Mayo Clinic in Rochester, Minnesota. By observing the Mayo brothers (William and Charles), she felt she was "learning the principles of practical surgery from the masters."

Her own surgical clinics attracted more than students. Karel Palent, a Czech journalist lecturing in the United States in 1908, reported on his attendance at a Van Hoosen clinic. Describing Bertha as short, stout, and plainly dressed, Palent wrote of her enormous skill and confidence. "She explains everything in a clear, pleasant, cheerful tone," Palent reported. He described Bertha as being "sure of her success...sure of her eye, her understanding and her hand" and "flushing" with intensity as she began the surgery. Comparing her technique to embroidery, Palent wrote that "the most skilled woman surgeon in the state of Illinois if the not the whole United States" continued to speak quietly, explaining each act and "working wonders" with her hands. Her reputation grew beyond gynecological surgery when she developed an operation that became known as a "buttonhole appendectomy." The surgeon explained that after making a half-inch incision below the patient's navel, "I insert one finger, locate the appendix, coax it out of the abdomen, and remove it." Her patients were not confined to bed and left the hospital on the fifth postoperative day.

For the first fifteen years of private practice, Bertha delivered infants in her patients' homes. She later wrote that she was "called when labor was evident and never left the patient until she had been delivered, whether it took hours or days." The long hours took its toll in exhaustion and time away from her other duties. For a time, she employed a young Swedish woman who was in training to be a nurse, Hannah Olson. Hannah acted as midwife so that Bertha could turn her attention to her additional work. But Bertha found that she was unable to concentrate, worried that some "obstetric incident might cost one or two lives if I were not watchfully waiting at my post."

Early twentieth-century births were accompanied by the use of pain medication during the early phases of labor. Chloroform, opium, cocaine, quinine, and others could not be used safely throughout the labor and delivery, because they inhibited muscle function or were dangerous for the fetus. Women experienced the full pain of childbirth, sometimes exacerbated by the use of forceps and resultant perinea tears. Post delivery recovery was long and complicated.

Bertha began to research the use of scopolamine-morphine anesthesia in childbirth. She saw that the anesthesia offered women a "return of more physiological births" and increased efficiency for the physician, and she worked on a protocol to make it safe. The dried rhizome was derived from a perennial plant in the *Solanaceae* family that was native to Bavaria and Austria-Hungary. Bertha referred to it as the "Elf from the Black Forest" that came to women's rescue to give relief from the pain of childbirth. She experienced even more resistance to the use of the anesthetic in obstetrics than she found with the use of surgical scopolamine. The medical establishment fought against the practice, citing earlier unstable forms of the drug as evidence of its danger to the infant.

Her efforts to win acceptance for scopolamine-morphine anesthesia were vindicated when she became the first, and only, woman to deliver a paper at the sixteenth International Medical Congress in Budapest in August 1909. Her presentation on scopolamine-morphine offered an opportunity for travel.

Alice and Sarah had returned from California several years before, and Alice was homeschooling her daughter. Overprotected and controlled by her mother, Sarah developed into a shy, lonely young woman. Alice worried about her daughter's development, writing in her diary that she "cared little for dress and cannot comb her own hair." She was "short and stout," "fond of eating," and "more clumsy than the other girls." Alice didn't see how lonely and unhappy the teenager was. Sarah's fondest memories were of times spent in Stoney Creek on the ancestral farm. She was more comfortable with the village children and farmhands than she was with the young people she was exposed to in Chicago and each year's return to Chicago brought protests. Bertha recalled Sarah exclaiming, "I don't want to go back to Chicago where nothing ever happens!" Sarah developed a strong bond with her grandmother, Sarah Taylor Van Hoosen, and the older woman understood her granddaughter's longings for the farm.

Alice and Bertha decided that to develop sophistication in the teenager, the four Van Hoosen women would embark on a grand tour of Europe with the International Congress in Budapest serving as the linchpin of the trip. Sarah worried that she would be homesick on her yearlong journey, and she captured images of Stoney Creek on her Eastman Brownie camera. Going house to house, the young woman asked the inhabitants to pose outside their homes, and she brought the fourteen pictures with her on her trip. She still treasured them fifty years later.

The Van Hoosen women visited New York City before setting sail on the Scottish steamship the *Ionia* on July 2, 1909. Their tour began in Scotland, where seventeen-year-old Sarah posed uncomfortably for a photograph in a kilt. Traveling on to the Netherlands, the group was unhappy with their lodgings and food, but they fell in love with the cleanliness and order of Germany. Their visit included Hildesheim, Cologne, Dresden, Frankfurt, Stuttgart, and Leipzig. In Munich, Grandmother Sarah sat transfixed by the Oberammergau *Passion Play*. Settling for a time in Vienna, the women took German language lessons, and Bertha visited the clinics of world-renowned surgeons Ernst Wertheim and August Bier. She was especially intrigued with Dr. Victor Schmieden's military surgical technique, and she was able to overcome the restriction against female attendance to observe his clinics.

In Budapest, Bertha felt there was an attempt to stop her from reading her paper at the International Congress of Medicine. She nervously rushed to the stage before her paper was properly introduced, but her dissertation on scopolamine-morphine was met with enthusiastic praise. Dr. Carl J. Gauss, the discoverer of "twilight sleep," encouraged Bertha to use the anesthetic in her obstetrical work.

The Van Hoosens returned to their travels and entered a cold, unwelcoming France in April. Bertha wrote that Paris "held no appeal" for her. The women headed to Italy, rode gondolas in Venice, stopped in Verona for a few hours, and stayed in a YMCA in Milan where they agreed they would rather not have to eat spaghetti ever again. Deciding to visit Cannes on the Riviera, Bertha was looking over maps when Alice asked where they were going and what was on the landmass nearby. Bertha answered that it was Algiers. When Alice dreamily said that she had always wished to see Algiers, Bertha began planning an unintended excursion into more exotic territories.

Traveling by boat and rail, the women visited Algiers, Constantine, Biskra, and Tunis. Finding no facilities on the North African trains, Grandmother Sarah used her farm-honed leg muscles to outrun turbaned Arabs to the rest stop lavatories. Sarah Taylor Van Hoosen saved the other three women from embarrassment or worse when they cheered the injury of a matador instead of the bull's defeat at an Algerian bull fight, dragging the others quickly from the stands. They stayed long enough in each venue to "get the atmosphere," and Bertha wrote of their interest in the exotic sights: the native dances, the henna-painted prostitutes, the camels, and Jewish bridal parties, as they spent afternoons at the watering trough at the outskirts of town.

When they returned to the continent, the Van Hoosen women traveled to Geneva and Berne, where Bertha observed the clinic of Nobel laureate and goiter specialist Emil Theodor Kocher. After another visit to Germany, the ladies began their westward trek with a visit to London and the clinic of Dame Louisa Aldrich-Blake, Britain's first female surgeon.

On their return to the United States in June 1910, Bertha and young Sarah became emotional at seeing the Statue of Liberty in New York Harbor. Their experiences had given them a renewed appreciation of their home country and its opportunities. Alice and Bertha believed they had attained their goal of broadening Sarah's interests and had prepared her to enter the University of Chicago.

Bertha's International Medical Congress experience bolstered her decision to use scopolamine-morphine (twilight sleep) on her obstetrical patients. The decision brought condemnation, mostly from male physicians. The twilight sleep method of childbirth took a great deal of the physician's time and incurred hospital expense. The progressive woman's clubs and female physicians of the early twentieth century took up the cause. Bertha became a leader of the twilight sleep movement with the publication of her 1915 book, *Scopolamine-Morphine Anesthesia*. In it, she explained the pharmacology of the drug, enumerated the five thousand surgical procedures she had "manipulated" using the controversial anesthetic, and explained its effect on her obstetrical patients. Its effects were controversial. While some patients fell asleep safely after the drug's introduction and woke after the successful delivery of their infant, others screamed and fought the nurses as they attempted to keep the patient in the hospital bed. To overcome these patients' excitement and create a safe environment for both the mother and nurses, Bertha designed a delivery bed. The bed resembled a large crib with canvas screens two and one-half feet high that restricted the patient's ability to climb out of bed. As labor progressed, the sectional bed was disjointed, and the mother's legs were placed in stirrups for delivery. While unconscious of what was going on around them, Bertha's patients were able to cooperate in the birth process and respond to the contractions of the uterus. While the medical establishment continued to obstruct its use, Bertha later wrote that the introduction of twilight sleep was as important to the advance of obstetrics as the introduction of maternal hygiene.

The book was not Bertha's first foray into professional writing. In the 1890s, she was approached by Margaret Rockhill, the business manager and owner of *The Medical Woman's Journal*, which was published in Ohio. The journal sought to give exposure to female doctors, but Bertha thought that promoting a woman's journal separate from the *Journal of the American Medical Association (JAMA)* would result in "retrogression" and a return to women-only medical schools and hospitals. She had graduated from a coeducational college and expected to be treated according to her own merits. She had heard of the difficulties suffered by the first female physicians but, in hindsight, felt that she had a poor understanding of the obstacles they faced. Her 1895 article, "A Case of Tubal Pregnancy," was published by *JAMA*, but her later attempts were routinely rejected. She collected rejections slips in a box she labeled "Jams from *JAMA*."

When the time came to publish her research on scopolamine-morphine, Bertha chose not to seek a publisher but to pay a printer to produce the book for her. After she placed the publication with the Chicago Medical Book Company, she saw weak sales. Ever the optimist, she felt that the book had done more for the author—organizing her research and solidifying her position—than for the reader.

After returning from Europe, Bertha was invited to join the staff of the Chicago Hospital for Women and Children. While attending staff meetings, she determined that the members of the board were using the hospital as a social outlet. She found that the trustees cared little for the staff and patients, and she let her displeasure be known. Her outspoken criticism of the hospital's trustees and board of managers resulted in her dismissal. Her friends and supporters Dr. Lindsay Wynekoop and Dr. Harriet Barrington Alexander met the same fate.

The three women heard that the board had decided to sell the hospital property and endow a ward in another institution. They demanded a meeting with the board, requested the board's resignation, and insisted that a new, completely female board and staff be assigned. They promised that the staff would be responsible for any new deficit, and they committed to liquidate the hospital's $6,000 deficit. Bertha secured the backing of nineteen female doctors who deposited $500 each in a trust fund.

The hospital needed a complete refurbishing. New beds, linen, and china were needed as well as modernized utilities and operating rooms. Three years later, the hospital was reconditioned and making money. Bertha was pleased to have an opportunity to care for her private and dispensary patients, but she was eager to find a surgical teaching position.

When she learned that Cook County Hospital was holding its first competitive examination for positions on the gynecological staff, she decided to enter the competition. She was interested to learn "what kind of showing I could make on paper." Her previous positions had been by appointment; even her license had not required a state board examination. Bertha was the only woman among the three hundred physicians who took the exam. When the results were posted at City Hall, she found that she had earned the highest grade and the coveted position of head of staff.

Before she was able to celebrate her success, Bertha received a visit from one of the other newly appointed hospital associates. Explaining that the civil service examiners had made a mistake, and she had not earned the highest grade, her visitor suggested that she voluntarily step aside and let a man take her place. Upset and ill over dinner that evening, Bertha listened to her sister's advice and approached the civil service board, appointment notice in hand. She learned that the earlier visit was a conspiracy by male physicians to deprive her of her position.

Bertha arrived to begin her service with not a chip but a "whole woodpile" on her shoulder. An intern led her to her first surgical patient, and she was informed that the woman had a large ovarian tumor and was already prepped for surgery. She refused to operate before examining the patient herself, and found the woman in an advanced stage of pregnancy. Bertha would write, "This experience taught me that I must walk gingerly."

Bertha was able to look back on her thirteen years of service in the Cook County Hospital as productive and fulfilling. She could operate two or more mornings a week on patients who were too poor to receive her services otherwise. Teaching allowed her to be altruistic alongside the staff and interns who "worked harder than I had ever seen doctors work" without pay. The two-thousand-bed county hospital was without prejudice, and all patients were treated alike. Guiding the surgical service of the male interns helped her to evaluate her own techniques as she observed them repeated in slow motion by her students. She had the opportunity to have "access to a superabundance of surgical material." She solidified her teaching technique by taking the interns through "the recognition of body tissues, the role of the assistant, and familiarization with surgical instruments and materials." Senior interns took part in surgeries.

The respect Bertha held for the hardworking interns was reciprocated by the male staff and students. When a young intern offered his room for the tired instructor to take a nap, Bertha "shuddered" at the thought of being found "asleep, like Goldilocks, on my intern's bed."

Dr. Mary McLean (left) and Dr. Bertha Van Hoosen

Sarah and Alice Van Hoosen Jones c. 1898

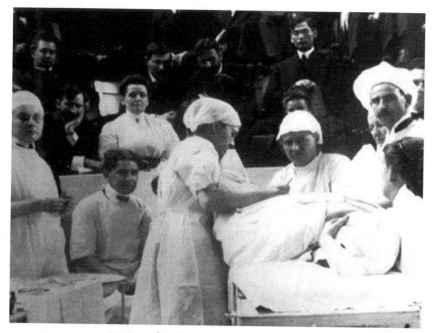

Dr. Bertha Van Hoosen, center, 1905

Sarah Jones, Scotland, 1909

From left: Bertha Van Hoosen, Alice Jones, Sarah Taylor Van Hoosen, North Africa, 1910

Bertha Van Hoosen, Chicago, 1910

Bertha Van Hoosen

Top row, from left: Bertha Van Hoosen, Alice Jones
Bottom row: Sarah Taylor Van Hoosen, Sarah Jones

SIX

U-boats of Sex Discrimination

⸺⸺⸺

The Van Hoosen household settled into a comfortable routine in the second decade of the 1900s. Sarah traveled by foot and cable car to her classes at the University of Chicago. Alice attended to the doctor's bookkeeping and running the house. While living in Chicago, Alice had a maid at a cost of seven to nine dollars per week.

The hired help served breakfast at 6:30 a.m. and a formal dinner when Bertha returned from work. Sarah wrote of enjoying the mealtime conversation, feeling she "had absorbed quite a medical education, learning the terminology though I might not know to just what the term referred." After dinner, Bertha frequently asked her sister if she would like to go to the theater, and the two ventured out into the night. The sisters were frugal and often walked as far as possible before taking a train downtown. They choose seats in the first row of the gallery, and their evening's entertainment usually cost sixty cents.

During the winter, Grandmother Sarah joined the household and spent her days reading the news from home in the *Pontiac Press Gazette*. She enjoyed being asked to cook one of her daughters' favorite childhood foods but otherwise was never asked to do any work.

Bertha moved to Chicago in an era when the Midwest city was a harbinger of the changes that would affect twentieth-century women. Chicago women had taken an active role in municipal life since before 1871, the year of the Great Chicago Fire. Although unable to vote, Esther Morris was elected Illinois' first female justice of the peace in 1870. Leading women intellectuals were able to join the Philosophical Society in the 1880s, and the Women's Christian Temperance Union found active members among the city's population. The Queen Isabella Association was founded in 1889, and its members were the archetype of the New Woman: middle class, educated, frequently holding a professional job, and challenging society's traditional view of her role. The group was active in the drive to bring the World Columbian Exposition to the industrial city. The Chicago Women's Auxiliary, an outgrowth of the city's women's clubs, competed with the "Isabellas" for influence over the Women's Building at the exposition. They wished to highlight philanthropy, while the Isabellas hoped to advance the cause of women's suffrage and equal rights.

In the medical world, Chicago was chosen by pioneering female physicians such as Sarah Hackett Stevenson, Mary Harris Thompson, and Lucy Waite as a place where "an ambitious new doctor could overcome the disabilities of her sex." Members of the Chicago Women's Club offered them support in return for professional expertise. The female doctors aided in accomplishing work on the club's women's and children's health-care agendas. In return, clubwomen raised funds to establish nursing schools and hospitals that accepted female doctors.

Other organizations also served middle-class, educated women: the Women's Trade Union League, the National Association of Colored Women's Clubs, and the National Council of Jewish Women.

Chicago was on the forefront of the suffrage movement. The National Woman Suffrage Association held a political convention in Chicago as early as 1880. Civil rights pioneer Ida B. Wells formed the Alpha Suffrage Group. The Suffrage Party of Cook County was formed in 1912 and dedicated to securing political equality for women. Chicago citizens saw numerous parades and demonstrations supporting the vote for women. Writer and public speaker Grace Wilbur Trout organized Suffrage Automobile Tours—ladies in sunbonnets drove cars bannered with signs reading "Votes for Women."

Just as the study of medicine was tied to a woman's maternal role by the female pioneers in the field, a woman's obligation to her family was emphasized in the issue of women's suffrage. Early proponents of female physicians stressed the unique blend of science and sympathy a woman brought to the doctor's role, "touching humanity in a way different from men." It was argued that voting helped mothers protect their children. In a pamphlet entitled *Why Women Should Vote*, Settlement House founder and activist Jane Addams wrote that the franchise was an extension of women's responsibility to run an efficient home and raise her children properly. Without a voice in community affairs, women could not have an effect on the communities where they raised their children or the schools their children attended.

Bertha moved comfortably among the leaders of the women's movement and supported Alice in her suffrage interests. After hearing the oratory of Elizabeth Cady Stanton and Mary Livermore, Alice became a "serious suffragist" and attended suffrage parades and speeches.

Both sisters supported Progressive Party presidential candidate Theodore Roosevelt, citing the former president's platform that included women's suffrage.

Bertha functioned in an increasingly feminine world. She was the head of a uniquely female nuclear family: her household included her mother, sister, and niece. Alice and her stepson, Horton, remained estranged, and young Sarah had only handymen, farmhands, and neighbors in Stoney Creek as male influences.

Bertha later wrote that "being a father to Sarah gave to my life a supreme motive," but she confessed that she received immense pleasure in being called "mother" by her "surgical daughters," the group of talented young women she trained in surgery. Bertha felt a "responsibility for and to my sex." She wrote, "Whenever I perform creditably, I set in motion courage, confidence, and optimism, from the smallest to the largest circles of my women colleagues, as a pebble dropped into a lake." She wanted there to be a new generation of female surgeons to replace her and her contemporaries, but she felt that female medical students were still hampered by bias. As a mentor, Bertha could be short-tempered and impatient, but she demanded no more of her surgical daughters than she did of herself. She loved to "dictate, to change people's habits and even their lives," and she admired the young women who could stand up to her. She wrote, "Like all mothers, I have carried them for so long I can see no fault in them, but I try never to omit an opportunity to perfect their technique or increase their knowledge." She reported training twenty young women. Many went on to successful careers in private practice; some devoted their lives to missionary work in China.

Realizing that having a female doctor refer a patient to a male surgeon would reinforce the idea that female physicians were not capable, Bertha began a twenty-five-year career as a "circuit surgeon." Traveling to thirty-six Midwestern towns, she visited forty-four hospitals on behalf of fifty-eight female physicians. Beyond adding to the confidence in female physicians in small towns, she felt that the experience helped to perfect her surgical technique. "It was necessary to leave patients in such condition that no trouble would develop after I departed," she wrote, "All bleeding must be prevented, no septic conditions must arise, the body tissues must not have too much strain upon them or the circulation cut off by too many sutures." Working with different nurses in each of the circuit cities, Bertha used a method she learned at the Mayo Clinic and could quickly explain. She never used more than three kinds of surgical needles: "a large, curved cutting needle for the skin, a small, curved, round needle for the deeper tissues, and a straight cambric needle for the appendix." Using a similar limited selection of suture material aided the nurse, she reported, "I never had to wait for sutures and never worried or confused the nurse."

When Alice was able to convince Bertha to accompany her to the cultural diversions the city offered, the sisters frequently enjoyed female entertainers. The beautiful Russian ballerina Anna Pavlova was among their favorites. Bertha reported watching eight consecutive performances of Pavlova in one week. The modern dancer Isadora Duncan held Bertha transfixed, unable to leave her Orchestra Hall seat after the barefoot dancer exited the stage. An autograph from the famous French actress Sarah Bernhardt, obtained in London, remains among her archived papers.

Bertha continued to chafe under the offensive of the "U-boats of sex discrimination" in her career. Her female patients still presented symptoms of marital abuses and she found herself the victim of unwanted advances from male patients. She became suspicious of any man asking for an appointment if she did not already treat female members of his family. She once had to call for a male medical student in an adjacent office to deal with a man who insisted on stripping for a "complete and thorough exam." She resented that men felt it was acceptable to tell off-color stories in her presence, often prefacing their remarks with "after all, you are a doctor."

Bertha's closest companions, after Alice, were other female doctors. She developed a close bond with Alice Lindsay Wynekoop, who she met when Wynekoop was a student at the Woman's Medical School of Northwestern University where Bertha taught embryology. She continued her relationships with Mary McLean and Rachel Carr, the older doctors who had helped her early in her career.

After establishing her Chicago practice, Bertha joined the Chicago Medical Society and the state and Cook County medical societies, but she was refused membership in her specialty's association, the Chicago Gynecological and Obstetrical Society. One of its members informed her that there was a clause in the bylaws expressly forbidding female membership.

The clause did not exempt the group from inviting Dr. Van Hoosen to speak at one of their meetings. The meeting was held at Chicago's prestigious University Club, and because women were not allowed above the second floor, Bertha and the visiting Michigan patient who was to share her surgical experience were prohibited from entering. To rally public opinion to the side of women, Bertha notified the city editor of the *Chicago Tribune*, and her grievance made the front page of the paper the next day. The attitude of the medical society, and the University Club, remained unchanged.

In 1876, the young doctor Sarah Hackett Stevenson was appointed as a delegate to the American Medical Association's conference in Chicago. Her credentials listed only her initials and no reference to her sex. Dr. Stevenson's appearance caused consternation among the attendees, but she was reluctantly granted membership in the all-male society. By the 1890s, the AMA was accepting women members, but as Bertha reported, they were largely ignored, and the annual conferences were uncomfortable for the female minority. She wrote of a conference when she was feeling exceptionally out of place and lonely when a pharmaceutical representative she recognized approached her. After escorting her to a private dining room and ordering champagne and lobster, the salesman suggested that they leave the conference for an afternoon in a "nice place in the country." Unable to hide her disgust, and feeling her face turn as red as the lobster, Bertha complained of feeling ill and left her suitor in a huff.

As more women joined the association, a tradition developed: the visiting female doctors were invited to a banquet put on by the female physicians in the conference's host city. In 1908, the Chicago doctors hosted the first dinner at the Millionaires Club. At that affair and each thereafter, one of the guests would be so moved by the collection of female doctors, and the solidarity expressed, that she made a motion for the formation of a women-only medical organization. Each year the idea was rejected soundly. Some saw female solidarity "as an obstacle to their professional success." Women were now accepted to major coeducational medical schools, and some had found varying degrees of success in private practice, teaching, and hospital positions. Discrimination was still rampant, but many of the women felt that identifying as a separate group would only delay gender assimilation. The all-women's medical schools served as a de facto organization of medical women, but their demise meant that the physicians were without an all-female support network. Bertha felt strongly that female physicians had to show loyalty to each other to advance the sex. She wrote, "Sex discrimination, like undersea raiders, strikes when least expected." Comparing female doctors to ships at sea, she continued, "Many are forced to reverse course or scatter widely." She wanted female doctors to travel in "a convoy," supporting each other and charting the way for those who followed.

Along with a small group of like-minded physicians, Bertha used the fiftieth anniversary of the founding of the Chicago Hospital for Women and Children by Dr. Mary Thompson to officially inaugurate the Medical Women's National Association (MWNA). Bertha took the position of the association's first president, and one of her postgraduate surgery students, Dr. Martha Welpton, became secretary-treasurer. Margaret Rockhill offered *The Medical Women's Journal* as the organization's official publication.

Bertha surprised herself with her zeal for organizing female physicians. She had always considered herself a strong individualist. She later wrote that her absorbing interest in group cooperation puzzled her, citing her independent childhood on the farm and the fact that she never held a student body office while at school.

The reaction of medical women throughout the United States was immediate and negative. The organizing action was condemned in petitions circulated in the medical community. Two years later, with the debate about the wisdom of female doctors organizing still raging, the

United States entered World War I. The American surgeon general issued a call to every physician in the country to apply for army service. Bertha reported that a majority of the five thousand practicing female doctors sent their applications to Washington. Each application was returned with a polite notice that women need not apply. Angered, the doctors circulated a petition this time voicing their indignation against the flagrant sex discrimination practiced by the federal government. The petition was forwarded to the women attending the 1917 meeting of the AMA in New York City. After deciding that the petition would carry more weight if submitted to the government by an organization representing female physicians, it was given to Bertha and the nascent MWNA. She traveled to Washington after operating for several days in New York. An exhausted Van Hoosen approached the Red Cross, asking for accommodations for female doctors eager to help in Europe outside of the military. Told there could be none, Bertha angrily wrote to Alice, "You would have thought they had to be refrigerated or something." Some adventurous American female doctors did find a way to serve in devastated Europe.

Bertha labored to advance the association's mission: "to fight unjust sex discrimination, to interest the lay public in the excellent quality of medical women's work, and to mass our efforts in advancing medical women." With renewed enthusiasm, she exercised her authority as the group's president to create an American Women's Hospital Committee to send relief to war-torn Europe. Bertha induced the National American Women's Suffrage Association, as well as other national and state women's associations, to financially support the effort. She appointed a New York doctor, Rosalie Slaughter Morton, as chairman. She wrote to Alice, "I hope this war work will be the making of the M.W.N.A. and make it grow more than it would in many years."

As Grandmother Sarah knitted a sock a day for American soldiers, the American Women's Hospital Committee grew its effort to provide medical care in Europe. Emily Barringer, a 1901 graduate of Cornell University School of Medicine and the first female ambulance surgeon, led a campaign to raise money for ambulances to be sent to Europe. She later successfully lobbied Congress to allow female doctors to serve as commissioned officers in the Army Medical Reserve Corps. At the war's end, the Young American Christian Association invited domestic and foreign women to gather in New York for a convention of distinguished women. At a gathering of members of the American Women's Hospital Committee units and visiting foreign female physicians, the International Medical Women's Association was founded.

In the April 1916 issue of *The Medical Women's Journal*, Bertha outlined the proposed scope and work of the association. She "recognized medical women as a class which has problems of its own that cannot be solved in the already existing medical societies." The new association promoted the interests of the five thousand female physicians practicing in the United States, even if they were not members. A directory was planned so that patients leaving one city could be referred to a woman physician in a new city. The association hoped to exert its influence in opening hospitals that were closed to women interns. Bertha included plans for loans, endowments, and scholarships for struggling female medical students and a fund for "aged or unfortunate women physicians." There would be no medical papers presented at conferences; meetings were open for "full and open discussions of any and all problems of interest to medical women alone."

The association had little money. Board members donated funds for the costs of printing and mailings, and Bertha donated the largest amount (thirty-five dollars). Dues were three dollars, with two dollars going to a subscription to *The Medical Women's Journal*. Bertha took over the journal's editorial duties. The relationship between the journal and the female doctors was difficult. Publisher Margaret Rockwell complained constantly of a lack of funds. She told Bertha that she could not afford to hire a salesperson for advertising but refused to tell the doctor the number of subscribers the journal had or its printing costs. Suspicious of Rockwell's accounting, Bertha and the association eventually severed relationships with the publisher.

Bertha's responsibilities at Cook County Hospital grew as she took over the surgical cases of men called into the services. She reported operating "from eight o'clock in the morning till eleven o'clock at night, stopping only for a one-half hour for luncheon and another half hour for supper."

In 1917, one of her interns, Dr. Louis D. Moorehead, and his former theological classmate, Patrick Mahan, S.J. joined the staff of the newly organized Loyola University School of Medicine. Moorehead became the acting head of the medical school, while Father Mahan became regent of the university. Loyola University was founded by the Members of the Society of Jesus, or Jesuits, in 1870. The medical school was instituted when Loyola acquired the Illinois Medical School, the Bennett and Reliance Medical Colleges, and the Chicago College of Surgery and Medicine after 1909. The school's first home was on S. Lincoln Street, later renamed Wolcott, directly across from the Cook County Hospital.

Loyola's growth coincided with the AMA efforts to reduce the number of medical schools by issuing evaluations and judging a school by the quality of its entering students, its profit status, and its physical plant. Loyola became one of the first medical schools to require at least one year of college prior to admission. The president of Loyola, John Furay, S.J. invited Bertha to become the school's acting head and professor of obstetrics. She realized that she would be the "first woman in the world" to hold that position in a coeducational medical school. She later wrote that the position was "the greatest tax upon my energy and resources." She realized that the two hundred senior students had had little opportunity to view the twelve deliveries needed for graduation. Calling upon her connections at the Chicago Hospital for Women and Children, she was able to prepare the senior class for graduation in three months. She was also responsible for fifteen unpaid teachers. At the time, doctors who took on teaching responsibilities were expected to teach, do research, and write for publication without a salary. The medical school teachers depended on their private obstetrical practices for support, with the frequent unplanned absences their confinement caseload demanded. Bertha often had to find a substitute at a moment's notice or teach the subject herself. With the support of Dean Moorehead and Regent Mahan, she worked diligently to "collect pathological material for microscopic study of diseases of the pregnant woman, to develop prenatal clinics, to secure motion pictures showing pathological deliveries, normal deliveries, and even birth in animals."

Bertha hoped to create a maternity hospital that provided affordable obstetric care to Chicago's middle class. She thought this institution would also provide teaching material for her students at Loyola. Her plans appeared to be coming to fruition when Frank J. Lewis, the owner of the Lakota Hotel, donated the hotel building at Thirteenth and Michigan Avenue to the Catholic Church. Cardinal George Mundelein wanted to use the fourteen-floor structure in the Church's effort to assist mothers, children, and families. The three hundred-bed hospital opened in January 1930 with the Sisters of Providence, a religious order of nuns from Montreal in charge. Hoping to curtail the rising practice of birth control among middle-class families, the Church sought to lessen the financial burden of childbirth for patients while offering the best possible obstetrical care. Bertha's hopes for teaching material for her students were not fulfilled until the late 1940s when Loyola's senior-year students were trained for six weeks in the hospital.

In 1918, Bertha accidently came upon a letter from the AMA awarding the medical school the coveted rating as a grade A medical school. The association's only recommendation was that Loyola "put a man in the head of the department of obstetrics." Speaking to Dean Moorehead, Bertha shared her delight in the institution's grade A status, but offered to resign so as to not hamper Loyola's future success, saying, "My work with you has been its own reward." Bertha recalled thirty years later that her former intern was astonished and told her that she was to be appointed the permanent head of obstetrics.

In a meeting with the university's president, Father Furay, Bertha was formally appointed to the position. "I know there is a prejudice against women," the Jesuit told her, "and we are prejudiced too, but it is for you and not against you." Bertha remained at Loyola until 1938.

SEVEN

A Halcyon Voyage

⎯⎯⎯⎯ ❧ ⎯⎯⎯⎯

*A*s a child, Sarah Van Hoosen Jones upset her mother by saying, "My, but I was lucky my father died." She did not mean to be cruel—she was referring to the fact that because of the early loss of her father, her aunt, Bertha Van Hoosen, stepped in as surrogate and became in all respects the girl's father. Sarah later wrote that no natural father could have done more for his offspring. As "father," Bertha was her sole supporter, the giver of gifts, and the one most generous with her affection.

Alice was often depressed and fearful that her daughter would be taken from her as her husband had been. Anxious and controlling, Alice did not allow Sarah to attend school or even learn to read or write. The little girl's requests to be taught to read received the reply, "Everyone in the world knows how to read, so you do not need to." When Alice brought the child home from California, she began to instruct her at home. At age nine, Sarah was enrolled in the Francis Parker School, which became associated with the University of Chicago a year later. To make up for lost time, Alice decided that Sarah should complete high school in three years and had the girl read Caesar before the ninth grade. Alice had Sarah read a year of Latin (Cicero) in one summer and, the following summer, had her read the six books of Virgil.

On the family's return to Chicago from their 1909 European tour, Sarah was enrolled in the University of Chicago to major in French and German. She felt herself a feeble student, made no friends, and was unhappy in the large city. Winter semesters were spent at Florida's first private university, Stetson. Sarah felt more comfortable in the all-girl school and kept scrapbooks of her friends and activities. The photographs show a plain young woman looking more content than in earlier images. She wrote happy letters home, even mentioning a fondness for a young man. College graduation brought an earnest discussion with her mother and aunt. Her guardians had decided that Sarah would follow Bertha into medicine, and plans were made for her to enter medical school. Sarah announced that she would study "premedic," but she wondered how long it would take to save enough from her private practice income to purchase her own farm. Bertha and Alice were dumbfounded. Bertha later wrote that she and her sister had "eyes that see not."

A discussion of the realities of twentieth-century farming followed, and it was determined that Sarah should earn a graduate degree from an agricultural college. Bertha brought Sarah to the University of Wisconsin–Madison, where she began work on a master's of science degree in animal husbandry. Her self-confidence grew as she developed from a lackluster young woman into an ambitious, successful student. Her mentor was Professor Leon Jacob Cole, a University of Michigan graduate and Yale professor before becoming the first head of the university's Department of Genetics. Noting Sarah's interests and abilities, Cole invited her to continue at Madison and work toward a doctorate. She remained in the University of Wisconsin an additional five years because of World War I; her services were needed to complete studies started by male students called to the military. In 1921, she became the first woman to earn a doctorate in genetics from the University of Wisconsin.

Grandmother Sarah had been able to care for herself and sojourn to the theater to see a movie several times a week. She hoped to attend her granddaughter's commencement service, but the ninety-one-year-old woman had fallen ill. Bertha wrote that when her mother became ill, "It seemed strange to all of us to be carrying trays of food to her, accustoming ourselves to the thought that she would never recover." Grandmother Sarah asked "Sally" (as the family called young Sarah) to parade around her grandmother's sickroom as if she were in the graduation ceremony. Grandmother presented the overcome young woman with the original deed to the family farm.

When Sarah Taylor Van Hoosen died on June 27, it was decided her granddaughter, Sarah, would return to Stoney Creek to prepare the eighty-one-year-old farmhouse for the final return of its mistress. Alone in her ancestral home, Sarah began to plan for her future, one that would take her from the city she disliked to the rural enclave she loved. The farmland was rented and tilled by local farmers. There was time to plan and study the dairy industry that she hoped to join. She became a full-time resident of Michigan, and Alice felt that her place was with her daughter. Alice took on the responsibility for the farm after her father died. She modernized the farm by updating the barns and adding a milk house and the area's first silos. In 1912, she replaced the dirt-and-plank floors of the large barn's basement with cement, and in 1914, she had a one-story tile barn constructed. The new barn had white plaster walls and was electrified, unlike the farmhouse she would join her daughter in.

Frequently called upon to mediate between renters and her mother, Alice resented the farm's hold on her time and attention. Alice confided in her diary that being responsible for the farm was like having a "chain around her neck." In her youth, she had lived in poverty in Saginaw in an attempt to remove herself from country life. Like her sister, she had fallen in love with Chicago, even announcing that when she died she wanted her "ashes broadcast over the Loop." Now she had to take up residence in Stoney Creek. Alice made plans to leave the city she loved.

Her conciliation was that the family planned to remodel the farmhouse. Alice loved to design and had shown a talent for decorating when she organized the home she shared with Bertha. The Van Hoosen women began to plan a new home on their ancestral land.

As Bertha approached sixty, she continued her challenging schedule. Her teaching obligations, hospital appointments, and private practice were demanding. She shared her practice with a former "surgical daughter," Dr. Maud Hall Winnett. Bertha's first cousin, Clara Stuart, worked as the office nurse. When Bertha developed bronchial asthma, her own physician advised spending winters in a warm climate. Instead, Bertha and Alice discussed making another extended foreign tour. They felt that Sarah would benefit from visiting dairy herds in New Zealand and Australia.

Bertha was eager to visit China and the women medical missionaries there. Her alma mater, the University of Michigan, had a long association with the kingdom. James B. Angell, the school president, had just returned from his assignment as US Minister to China when Bertha attended the university. At the close of the World Exposition in New Orleans in 1885, the government of China donated its elaborate display to the Ann

Arbor school. In the 1890s, the University Medical School opened its doors to Chinese women who returned to their native land as medical missionaries. In 1914, the university began the Barbour Scholarships for Oriental Women. Several of these Chinese students had trained with Bertha as surgical daughters. Bertha's mentor, Mary McLean, had made several missionary trips to China and hoped to locate there permanently.

Preparations for the trip began in earnest. The *JAMA* reported that Bertha announced her travel intentions at a dinner given in her honor in November 1921. As she would not be living in Chicago on their return, Alice sold the house her late husband built and packed their household belongings for the move to Stoney Creek. Bertha arranged for an indefinite leave of absence from Loyola Medical School and a substitute attending obstetrician at Cook County Hospital.

Their departure date was changed when Bertha's gallbladder ruptured in July 1922. She recovered quickly and operated again after just one month, but she decided they would begin their adventure in October. Bertha booked passage for Hawaii.

The group which now included her cousin, Clara Stuart, left San Francisco with second-class tickets to Honolulu. Bertha kept meticulous notes of every penny spent and recorded renting a furnished bungalow for fifty dollars a month.

The ladies reveled in the variety of fresh fruit available. Their new home had papaya trees and banana stalks in the yard. They ate pineapple, breadfruit, and mangoes for the first time. Enjoying the temperate climate and the absence of mosquitoes, Bertha made a "fearsome trip" on a surfboard, "beheld" her first volcano, and visited a leper colony. The ladies enjoyed going to the harbor and watching the passenger ships arrive and depart. The arriving tourists were feted with leis, and the departing guests were sent off to the sound of Hawaiian bands and the "pleading strains of Aloha Oe." Bertha appreciated the racial tolerance she found among the natives. She was invited to give a lecture at a Honolulu prenatal clinic, and she used the peel of a pomelo, a "fruit resembling a very large grapefruit" and a tangerine to demonstrate the relation of the fetal head to the mother's pelvis in labor.

Soon after her arrival, Bertha encountered a former patient at the Honolulu post office. Exclaiming "the Lord has sent you," the woman explained that she had been told that she needed an appendectomy. Bertha performed the surgery in Queen's Hospital, earning "enough money to pay for my passage to China."

After five weeks in Hawaii, the women sailed for China by way of the South Seas, stopping for a day at the still primitive Fiji Islands. In New Zealand, Sarah carried her Brownie camera into the countryside, and her many photographs documented the nation's thriving dairy industry. Bertha visited a home run by the Plunket Society. Started in 1907 by Dr. Frederick Truby King, the community-based organization encouraged breastfeeding, an issue in which Bertha was becoming more involved.

After an uncomfortable voyage across the Tasman Sea, the group spent three weeks in Australia. Bertha enjoyed the professional courtesy and hospitality of the surgeon Sir Alexander McCormick, observing him operate and visiting his Sydney home. The day included a ride on his magnificent yacht in the Sydney Harbor.

Sailing on the Japanese vessel, the *Yoshira Maru* from Sydney, the women enjoyed a "dream voyage," "drifting from one island to another" on the Coral and South China Seas. On a stop at Thursday Island, they saw pearl divers and shop after shop of cabinets filled with the beautiful harvest. Their ship docked twice in the Philippines before arriving in Hong Kong.

In 1923, Hong Kong was a British colony and a free port where merchandise could be exchanged without paying import duties. Bertha and her travel companions encountered the Chinese people as they departed the ship and made their way to the European community near Victoria Park. The early twentieth century was a dangerous time to visit the Oriental kingdom. Memories of the slaughter of the antiforeigner Boxer Rebellion were still fresh, and a new threat, an anti-Christian movement, had recently been launched. Protestant and Catholic denominations were active in educational and medical work and were seen as threats to traditional Chinese values. The religious communities were weaker targets that could be exploited by anti-imperialist political parties.

The Van Hoosen women knew of the dangers and heeded advice to wait safely in a hotel in the foreign enclave until instructions arrived from Mary Fulton, the American physician who was to be their hostess in Canton. Fulton had established the Kwangtung Medical School for

Women under the auspices of the Board of Foreign Missions of the Presbyterian Church in the United States. In 1905, the school was expanded and renamed the Hackett Medical College for Women. Bertha was to lecture and operate during her visit there. Reaching the school meant travel by train, rickshaw, and sedan chair. When they arrived in the capital of the Guangdong Province, the women were met by workers from the school. They were presented with the sedan chairs, and the women climbed aboard and felt themselves hoisted onto the shoulders of young men. The nervous travelers were carried through narrow lanes that were more like tunnels than streets. Bertha reported occasionally discovering a hand pulling on the sedan side curtain and a "curious Chinese face peering into mine."

The group left Canton by train. Bertha was eager to visit with fellow Michigan native Gertrude Howe. Howe spent fifty-six years in China after answering a call by the Methodist Church to minister to the Chinese. She adopted four Chinese girls and educated several others. Two of the girls, Dr. Ida Kahn and Dr. Mary Stone, were among the first Chinese women to become medical doctors after attending the University of Michigan Medical School. Dr. Stone was the daughter of a Chinese teacher who had asked Howe to direct his daughter's education. Dr. Kahn was the rejected daughter of an upper-class family. A negative horoscope had predicted that the infant girl would bring grief and dishonor to any family she was betrothed to. Destined for slavery or worse, the child was saved and adopted by the missionary. In 1923, the women were serving their people in Shanghai and Nanchang.

Stone (whose Chinese name was Shi Meiyu) established and ran two hospitals before building the Bethel Mission near Shanghai. The travelers visited Stone and found thriving schools, a hospital, a center for training nurses, and an orphanage. Bertha called the mission "a little city in itself," and she praised Stone's efforts to save "bodies and souls, to bring habits of health...to develop character and ambition by pleasure and faith."

During the Van Hoosen tour, Dr. Kahn was running a hospital compound in Nanchang. After arriving by train, the women were met by sedan chairs and firecrackers. Their noisy procession through the town brought hundreds of Chinese into the streets to see the foreigners go by. Along with a beautiful rose garden, Kahn and her adoptive mother, Miss

Howe, ran a hospital compound that impressed Bertha with its "order and cleanliness."

While operating with Dr. Kahn, Bertha noticed a large platform with row upon row of sparkling, two-gallon brass teakettles filled with water for sterilization. She noticed a large American-made sterilizer in the corner of the operating room and was was told it could not be used without gas and served to remind the Chinese of what they needed to work toward. A brass kettle became one of Bertha's first "souvenirs" of her stay.

In Kiukiang, Bertha reunited with Dr. Li Yuin T'sao. She met T'sao when Bertha's mentor, Mary McLean had requested that she take on the young Chinese woman as an assistant in the Willard Hospital in Chicago. T'sao had attended Northwestern University and the University of Michigan. Her medical degree was from Chicago's Rush Medical College, and she interned in New York City's Bellevue Hospital and the New England Hospital for Women and Children. Bertha felt that no other Chinese woman had come to America for her medical education and returned to her native land so "well equipped." In Kiukiang, Bertha spent long days in the surgical theater with Dr. T'sao and operated on as many as fifteen patients in a day.

As impressive as the American-trained Chinese women doctors were, Bertha could see that their countrywomen suffered from the tradition of female inferiority at all levels of society. Women were poorly educated and had little control over their lives; a woman's destiny was determined by her ability to produce male offspring. Betrothed as infants, Chinese girls married soon after reaching puberty and moved to the mother-in-law's home. Reporting in *The Medical Woman's Journal* in December 1923, Bertha wrote, "The girl is given to understand that she is of no importance, and the only thing that can justify her existence is to be able to bear a child, and of course it must be a male child."

She was horrified at the tradition of foot-binding, the maiming of young girls' feet to fit a rigid idea of female beauty. Except for the big toe, all the toes of the girl, usually age six, were bound under the foot. The heel and toes were then bound together, creating a "lily foot." Women with bound feet were rarely seen in public, because walking, especially trying to climb stairs, was extremely painful.

In Peking, she called on a concubine of the "Little Emperor" with her host, Dr. Emma Martin, and visited a "Door of Hope" home where she met young women trying to leave a life of prostitution. As the Chinese did not drink cow's milk, poor women went "from door to door of the well-to-do" to allow babies and ailing adults to nurse on their breast milk. In China, Bertha saw patients suffering from osteoporosis, and she recoiled from the tradition of placing newborns in a sack containing several cups of sand instead of cleaning and dressing the infant.

Traveling near Peking, Bertha saw a woman standing on her roof, "screaming at the top of her lungs." She was told that the woman was displeased with how she was treated by her husband and was letting the world know. She would continue until her voice failed her. Bertha could understand the woman's frustration.

The Chinese women were fascinated with the female foreigners who traveled around their country unescorted. While visiting a patient with Martin, Bertha questioned why the patient laughed through her examination. Martin explained that it was the patient's first experience of Western women, and she thought they were "funny." A surprised Bertha was told that she was funny and that her hair looked "like a rat nested in it." She had "shameless breasts, sticking out on your chest, instead of being bandaged close to the body." Worst of all were her feet, said to "look like gunboats."

Bertha understood the curiosity the native women exhibited. More than once, she felt a hand traveling up her skirt to discover what she had on underneath. Dr. Martin had told Bertha she had once stripped to her skin to allow the women to exam the inner layers she wore.

The women fell in love with Peking. They found moats filled with lotus blossoms surrounding the Forbidden City, climbed the Great Wall, and explored the art in the Summer Palace. They sat in parks and watched "the passersby; young men, with their ankle-length, delicately tinted, high-necked coats; young women with their gray trousers and kimono-like upper garments...men wearing pigtails; women with elaborate glossy puffs and decorative hairpins." Bertha addressed the graduating class of the Peking Woman's Medical College and offered to assume the surgical work at the Sleeper Davis Hospital so that its head, Dr. Francis Heath, could take a much-needed rest. She had the opportunity to instruct the

Chinese interns in surgery and oversaw one student's first cesarean section. One young woman, Dr. Knei Chen Shen, later served an internship under Bertha at the Frances Willard Hospital.

The ladies were not as fond of Chinese food as they had been of Hawaii's fruit. Unable to eat watermelon seeds as the Chinese did, Bertha acquired a taste for many forms of sprouts. They discovered "tea eggs"—eggs boiled in strong tea with cracks in the shell that allowed the tea flavor to permeate the egg. They were introduced to soup with tiny pigeon eggs dropped into it before serving. In Shanghai, they had butter made from water-buffalo milk. Bertha called it "white as lard but of very delicate taste." While they agreed to never consume any uncooked food or unboiled water, Alice became dangerously ill with an intestinal infection on their second visit to Peking. Bertha determined that the culprit was the ice cream that she thought had been cooked before freezing. Alice hovered near death for several weeks but finally responded to treatment by Dr. Heath.

Though still weak, Alice joined her fellow travelers as they boarded a Japan-bound vessel at Tientsin. Bertha described the voyage to Kobe as "halcyon," and she was eager to see Japanese people. The group visited Kyoto and Nara before arriving in Yokohama. They passed through "groves of feathery bamboo and small lakes pink with thickly growing lotus blossoms." They unpacked and admired their Oriental purchases: jade, brass, Chinese bowls with rice patterns, vases, clothing of silk, and six Chinese rugs.

The next morning, the women took a short train ride to Tokyo and were entering the Imperial Hotel lobby when Bertha heard "the noise of noises. It came from above and below; it closed in on all sides." Crying "earthquake," Sarah grabbed her companion's arms and pulled them from the shaking building. They reached the door just in time to see a six-story stone building across the street collapse. Alice became hysterical. As they clung to each other and uttered "unintelligible words," the women felt another movement. Bertha noticed the Japanese people around them squatting, and she ordered her sister and the others to do the same. Bertha timed the aftershocks "as we do labor pains" and moved the frightened group to a grassy plaza in front of the hotel.

The women were caught in what became known as the Great Kanto Earthquake of September 1, 1923. The seismic scale of the time only went to 6, but based on the degree of damage, it is believed that it would have registered as high as 8.3. Because the quake struck at noon as lunches were being cooked over open fires in the mostly wooden city, fires raged instantly. An hour after the quake hit, Alice noticed smoke rolling out of the buildings surrounding the plaza. They saw Japanese filling the streets, some covered with blood and pulling belongings in carts. They were advised to go to a park for the night, and the local police supplied blankets. Bertha wrote that they spread their blankets on the ground "not to sleep but to watch the fire and listen to the poor people who were pacing the park looking for lost relatives." The death toll was more than one hundred thousand.

In the morning, the Americans returned to their hotel and "were amazed to see it still standing." The hotel was a Frank Lloyd Wright structure whose main building materials were poured concrete, concrete block, and carved oya stone. Cantilevered floors and balconies provided extra support as did tapered walls. After receiving rations for breakfast, the women spent the day sitting in the hotel's vestibule, occasionally running into the plaza during a strong aftershock. Other hotel guests ventured out to gather information, and the group learned that Yokohama had been destroyed. They had left that city on the last train to make it out safely. Railroads and bridges were gone. The Tokyo docks were damaged, and all available ships were on route to Yokohama to aid the more devastated city. They met an American whose wife had stayed behind in the Grand Hotel in Yokohama, and he was desperate for news. A young American teacher had a ticket for a boat to the States and was frantic to get there.

A Eurasian gentleman from Kobe announced that he would attempt to reach that city in the morning, and he agreed to take the American survivors with him. After another fitful night, the man from Kobe, Mr. Jonas, told the women that their escape from the city would be difficult. It may take as long as three days, and he could not guarantee success. Bertha reasoned that food would become scarce if they stayed in Tokyo and was concerned about the sanitary conditions. She could see that Alice was getting weaker, but she felt that they must make the attempt to leave the city.

A group of fourteen began their escape. Jonas commandeered several cars and a few gallons of gasoline. They saw the ravaged city for the first time. The fire had destroyed structures for miles around. They passed damaged automobiles and street cars, tangled wires, and twisted girders. The road was impassable after two miles, and the group was forced to walk. Bertha described the feeling of a Turkish bath as they struggled by smoldering fires. They were joined by thousands of refugees, most struggling with carts and bundles of possessions. Clara had to support Alice, and they worried that she would eventually need to be carried.

After three miles, they reached the outskirts of the city. They climbed aboard an electric car for a ride of twenty minutes, and rain fell as they walked the next four miles. Jonas found a shed for shelter, and the exhausted group sat on mats on the floor. Two of the men left to scavenge for food and came back with wine and tins of pineapple, pears, and lobster. After crossing a river on a bridge made of boats, the hike became more difficult as their path went through fields and uneven terrain. When they finally reached a train station, Bertha watched as a train eased out of the station. Refugees filled every space, "hanging like barnacles to the sides of the cars." The group was afraid of being crushed and hung back, waiting for the crowd of refugees to diminish.

Just before midnight, the group boarded a train and arrived at a junction at 2:00 a.m. They dropped to the cement floor at the station and rested fitfully until 4:00 a.m. when Mr. Jonas announced that he had found a train that would take them straight to Kobe. For thirty hours, the group sat leaning against each other like the throngs of Japanese who filled the train. Bertha was amazed by the behavior of the mass of people. No one pushed or shoved; each cared for the other. As the train stopped at what seemed like one-hour intervals, balls of cooked rice, sandwiches, water, apples, and even sake were handed into each window by unseen donors. The trip took them from Tokyo across Japan to the western coast, along the coast for miles, and again across Japan to get to Kobe.

The women thanked Jonas and were welcomed by an American who let them use his hotel room. Their clothing was torn and filthy, and the women did not leave the hotel room for nine days until replacements could be found at a relief center. Their passage home was booked on the

Empress of Asia for September 15. Once at sea, they learned that Kobe was struck by a tidal wave.

Newspapers worldwide reported the catastrophe, and lists of the travelers who were dead or missing filled the pages. The *Chicago Tribune* announced that Chicago physician Bertha Van Hoosen and her traveling companions had survived the Great Kanto Earthquake.

Sarah Van Hoosen Jones (second from left), University of Wisconsin–Madison, 1918

Sarah Van Hoosen Jones c. 1933

The Van Hoosen farmhouse under construction c. 1926

Bertha Van Hoosen at Mary Thompson Hospital, Chicago

Bertha Van Hoosen, Chicago Women's Club, Chicago

Petticoat Surgeon (1947)

Alice and Bertha, Stoney Creek, Michigan

"When I was born the door that separates the sexes had opened scarcely more than a crack, but it has been my privilege, my pain, and my pleasure to pound on that door...and finally to see it, although not wide open, stand ajar."

EIGHT

Creating Shangri-la

———∞∞∞———

*T*he new home that Bertha, Alice, and Sarah were planning for their ancestral land in Michigan was literally their dream home. They had been thinking about the home they would one day create for so long that they had fixed ideas of what the house should be like.

Before their trip to the Orient, the women had established an orchard and surrounded the large lot with a stone wall. When construction was to begin, the first major decision was the structure's placement. The 1840 farmhouse that Alice and Bertha were raised in, and that Sarah knew so well from her childhood, sat on a knoll overlooking the farmland. Its once-pristine view was cluttered with outbuildings. For the new home's location, they chose the site of their pioneer forefather's gristmill. It sat atop a hill that overlooked Stoney Creek and the man-made millrace that once brought water to turn the mill's wheel. Rather than build a new home, the women elected to move the original farmhouse to the new position and create a low, long structure "following the rise of land above the creek even as our ancestors had built their cabins on such a rise."

To accomplish their plan, the Van Hoosens hired a Detroit architectural firm known for its Early American designs that fit the women's tastes and desires. The new home preserved the original farmhouse parlor, kitchen, and bedchambers on the second floor. New extensions created an entrance hall, parlor, and dining room along with a large library on the first floor. A winding oak staircase led to a balcony view of the library. The small bedchambers over the front gable were replaced by one large bedroom, and two new rooms were added over the extensions. As builders, they hired two Stoney Creek residents—one a carpenter, the other a mason—and contracted an hourly rate.

The project took fifteen months to complete. Some building materials were reclaimed from structures torn down for the home site.

A red brick smokehouse had bricks reused in the home's fireplaces, while the hand-hewn timbers of a horse barn became the beams in the library's vaulted ceiling. The black walnut flooring in the library was taken from Uncle Nathaniel Millerd's home, the first frame house built in Stoney Creek and the house the Van Hoosen women lived in while supervising the home's construction. The home was furnished with the furniture from the Van Hoosen's Chicago home and family heirlooms. Grandmother Sarah had owned a complete set of haircloth furniture dating from 1870. The sofa and matching chairs now took pride of place in the library. A chest of drawers carried from upstate New York by the Taylor settlers sat in the parlor. The property's original parchment land grant, signed by President James Monroe in 1824, hung above it.

To complete the decoration of the home, the women needed to reorder some of their Oriental purchases destroyed in the Japanese quake. Four eight-by-ten rugs of taupe, pink, and blue were handmade especially for the home in a Peking factory. A brass teakettle of the type used for sterilization in Chinese operating rooms sat in the nook of an oval window midway up the winding staircase. The front door would be guarded by two six-hundred pound, three-hundred-year-old carved stone Ming lions acquired by missionary Alice Barlow Brown, MD, on Bertha's request. At the lions' feet lay a millstone in homage of the profession of their Taylor forebears.

A firm in Texas executed a fire screen for the library's fireplace. The three-section screen, designed by Alice, honored her parents. The center section's ironwork was an image of Mount Moriah, the large hill that looked down on Stoney Creek Village. One side panel depicted the young Joshua Van Hoosen, standing in the California gold fields, pick in hand. The other side panel portrayed Sarah Taylor Van Hoosen as an octogenarian, standing near a farm silo.

Other decorations were gifts from Bertha's grateful patients: a painted view of Venice by an artist whose wife she had performed a difficult hysterectomy on, a cuckoo clock from a couple whose child was born with Bertha's help, a bas-relief plaster of the Greek image of hospitality from a surgical patient, and a walnut piano given in lieu of payment by a lady from the "world of clandestine sports."

Bertha called the lovely new home her "Shangri-la, the place where, by passing room to room, I revitalize experiences that have come to a country-born woman who for fifty years has poured her energies into the cast of a medical career."

Bertha's professional life brought her back to Chicago and a rented room in the Chicago Women's Club. She wrote that its "modern blond furniture and fresh decorations fixes my attention on present day troubles and duties." Her "present day duties" included her work at Loyola University and Cook County Hospital, her private obstetrical and surgical practice, her involvement with the renamed American Women's Medical Association, AWMA, and her numerous speaking engagements.

As the decade unfurled, she continued to throw herself into work on social issues. Cook County Hospital coworker Rachelle Yarrow had made a name for herself promoting social hygiene and sex education. Bertha's beliefs on the subject evolved over time. In a talk to the Women's City Club in 1912, she responded negatively when the mothers in the room asked her if they should share sexual information with their children. She told them to "let them find out the way nature lets man find things out." Five years later, she told another group that parents should teach their children "the plain facts of sex matters instead of making a mystery of them." She was invited to speak to girls' high school classes and prided herself in not shocking the young women or having any faint during her talk.

Bertha still lived in a feminine world and did not get involved romantically with any man after her college days. She was most likely still a virgin. In 1929, she wrote in *The Medical Woman's Journal,* "It is only the exceptional person who does not believe that the most normal life for any woman is to be married and have children," but the public consensus was still that medical women should not marry. In London, a discussion proposed that "the woman medical student should be denied a medical education unless she is willing to renounce matrimony." Bertha felt that marriage and childrearing helped a female doctor to give better service in pediatric and obstetrical specialties. In a *Medical Woman's Journal* article titled "Marriage—An Asset or a Handicap to the Medical Woman," Bertha wrote, "The argument is not that a woman should have a right to marriage and a career, but more than that, she should have a right to become a part of everything in life that will enrich her mind and body, develop her character, and help to make her do her part in the world's work in as big a way as possible."

Her gynecological practice brought her into discussions with her patients about sexual relations, but her writings show a naïveté about the emotions and reactions of the sexually active female. She wrote that the female was passive in the sexual act and did not have a "physical urge for action and the sense of relief that comes to the male." As a reference, she cited the work of Richard van Krafft-Ebing. His book, *Sexual Psychopathy: A Clinical Forensic Study*, claimed that the purpose of sexual desire was procreation, and any form of recreational sex was a perversion of the sex drive. Bertha explained that women were "endowed with greater self-control than the man; a finer sense of responsibility to the race; and hereditary love of service to humanity." She carried her theory further and created a "tempest in a teapot" when she advocated that "women, not men should be the sex aggressors." In a talk before the Eugenics Education Society, she explained, "We would be a great deal nearer solutions of the problem of the human family" if women chose their mates.

She loathed the reality of women bearing children every year. She remembered her father calling attention to the cemeteries where the husband's grave was centered among those of his three or four wives, "mute witnesses of maternal crucifixion on the cross of too-frequent childbearing." She reported her father saying, "I wouldn't treat any of my critters like that!"

During Joshua's time, there was no public discussion of contraception, but while birth control was not publically accepted, it was privately practiced. Early methods included sponges, rubber sheaths, and withdrawal. Before 1920, feminist groups considered birth control a part of the women's rights movement, and its attachment to the cause caused birth control to appear a radical idea. During the 1920s, the movement became less concerned with women's rights and more with health and population control. Women were at last able to discuss their marital relations with their doctors, and Bertha recorded advising her patients to abstain from sex. She felt that "mutual, voluntary, marital continence" was admirable as a considerate and modern form of self-control. She did not mention advising patients on external birth control choices.

Beyond her private practice, more contemporary views of the contraception debate prevailed. At a 1930 meeting, the American Medical Women's Association (AMWA) resolved that "contraceptive counseling was a wholly proper medical function." The resolution was adopted in Detroit in 1931.

Bertha continued to have her emotional needs met by her sister, Alice, and niece, Sarah. As Sarah began her farming venture in Michigan, Bertha made frequent trips to Stoney Creek.

Sarah Jones had begun her efforts with a flock of single-comb white leghorn hens. She moved into the poultry house and slept on a cot to care for the hundreds of baby chicks. Bertha watched Sarah and wondered if cleaning chicken coops was "the best use of all the degrees she had acquired." Once the egg production was established, Sarah hired a poultry man and turned her attention to the dairy side of the business. She took over the certified milk business run by the last renter and was now the owner of fifty head of Holsteins.

Bertha frequently became involved in the medical care of the farm animals. When some chickens died of the coccidiosis, a parasitic disease, Bertha suggested putting iodine in their drinking water, which turned their white feathers a brilliant yellow. She treated an umbilical hernia in a calf by bandaging the animal with "bolts of adhesive tape." Watching the treatment of the dramatic disease of puerperal paresis, a condition where a newly delivered cow appears suddenly paralyzed, inspired Bertha to find a way to treat women displaying high blood pressure, the precursor of toxemia in expectant mothers. Stricken cows were injected with air into the udder; Bertha expressed secretions from the pregnant woman's breast as soon as her blood pressure began to rise.

Seeing that Sarah prevented goiter in calves by giving expectant cows iodized salt, Bertha gave iodine to pregnant patients and instructed them to give an occasional iodine preparation to the growing child.

By the 1930s, the farm had become a successful concern. Sarah reported, "The sale of certified milk was the lifeblood of the farm's economics, enhanced by the sale of livestock." Stoney Creek Village now consisted of twenty households, most headed by Van Hoosen farm employees. Alice had worried that her daughter would be isolated, but Sarah's life included membership in a local professional women's club and service as president of the Washington Farmer's Club. She was active in the county, state, and national Holstein-Friesian associations and won numerous awards for her herds. Sarah developed a relationship with Michigan's agricultural college, Michigan State, followed the latest in farming practices, and used its help to organize her business bookkeeping. In 1933, she was recognized as a master farmer by *Michigan Farmer Magazine*.

As the decade continued, her reputation spread. The owner of a Venezuelan ranch visited the farm and purchased eight young sires and three females. One female calf was shipped to the Inter-American Institute of Agricultural Science in Costa Rica in an attempt to build a Holstein herd.

Sarah opened a farm store and office in a recently purchased and remodeled village building. A young woman named Alice Serrell was hired to manage it. The "Sign of the Black and White Cow" sold farm products as well as consignment items from area women. Cookies, jams, jellies, and soft goods filled the store's shelves, while cattle buyers and other businessmen met with Sarah in the building's office. City dwellers seeking a country respite, hikers, and school field trips kept the retail store busy year round.

Alice enjoyed her return to country life. She was hostess to numerous farm potluck picnics and helped organize family reunions for the extended Taylor descendants. In celebration of the Michigan constitution's one hundred years in 1935, she wore her mother's nineteenth-century clothing and rode in her father's original surrey in Rochester's Jubilee Parade. With great pride, Alice and Sarah attended the 1935 memorial for Alice's grandmother, Sarah Boardman Taylor, conducted by the Daughters of the American Revolution in the pioneer cemetery on the hill above the farm. In 1948, the Van Hoosen Farm was recognized as a Centenary Farm (a farm held in direct lineal decent in a family for one hundred years or more) by the Michigan Historical Commission.

As Stoney Creek neighbors and friends became aware of Bertha's frequent visits to the farm, many asked if she would see them as patients during her stays. A biweekly Stoney Creek practice soon developed. Bertha left Chicago on Friday for a three-hundred-mile bus trip. Using Sarah's automobile on Saturday mornings, she operated in Detroit or

Pontiac and returned to the farm to hold office hours on Sunday morning, when she would see as many as thirty patients. Her grandmother's 1840 front parlor became the doctor's examination room. Medications were delivered via a small window in the maid's quarters. Bertha wrote that she established the Stoney Creek practice so that when she left Chicago, she would have a "full-fledged practice to continue instead of retiring." Health problems in 1939 and 1940 forced her to discontinue the Michigan practice.

Alice visited Chicago for cultural stimulation and to spend time with her sister. While her funds continued to support Alice, Sarah, and the farming venture, Bertha still depended on her sister for emotional sustenance and affection. Once the house was completed and decorated, Alice had turned her attention to horticulture, and she transformed the farmhouse's yard into a showcase garden. She wrote a friend that given the choice of a new plant or a loaf of bread, she would choose the plant.

In April 1929, Bertha and Alice booked passage on the Spanish liner the *Alfonso XIII* to attend the Medical Women's International Congress in Paris. Because they missed Spain, Portugal, and the west coast of Italy on the 1909 trip, the sisters extended their journey for three months.

Bertha brought with her a letter from the regent of the Loyola University School of Medicine requesting an audience with the pope for the American sisters. The request was granted, and Bertha and Alice were to visit the Vatican on Holy Monday, the day after Easter. After reviewing directives on how to dress for the audience, which included wearing mantillas, Bertha realized she did not have the required black shoes. Not wanting to waste money on shoes she did not need otherwise, she bought a pair of shiny black rubbers. After Alice mocked her choice, Bertha retorted that the rubbers were no funnier than the mantillas. To save funds, Bertha insisted on traveling to the Vatican by streetcar rather than taxi. After getting lost in Rome for a time, the women arrived for the audience and waited several hours before Pope Pius XI made his appearance. Bertha was relieved that her rubbers were covered as she knelt for the pontifical blessing. As she kissed the pope's ring and observed him for the remainder of the visit, Bertha felt that she had met a "fine public servant."

Taking the opportunity to shop internationally for more decorations for their Stoney Creek home, the sisters looked for a tapestry to hang on the library's story-and-a-half fireplace. Finding that even the Spanish shawls were made in China, they discovered a pleasing specimen in the Pitti Palace in Florence. They were frustrated by the language barrier and vendors unwilling to part with prized tapestries. The proprietor of their hotel came to their rescue, and a replica was found. Bertha gushed about the gentlemen of Florence.

It had been nineteen years since Bertha attended the international medical congress in Budapest. The Paris meeting, organized by international medical women, whetted her appetite for attending more. Two years later, Alice and Bertha sailed from New York to the Isthmus of Panama to attend the Pan-American Association meeting. She was the first woman invited to address that association's conference. Bertha's paper on corrective obstetrics reported on fifty cases and described the Pubiotomy procedure. (Pubiotomy, the surgical enlargement of a pelvis too small to allow a normal delivery, is now rarely performed in developed nations.) Bertha explained that the surgery corrected the deformity, while a cesarean section, the more commonly used procedure, did not ensure future normal deliveries.

On the return trip, the sisters took the opportunity to sightsee. They visited Cristobal, "gay Havana," and Guatemala before arriving in New Orleans in time for Mardi Gras. Five years later, Bertha was unable to convince Alice to accompany her to another medical conference in Stockholm, and she traveled instead with a large group of female physicians from all over the United States. Their ship, the *Gripsholm*, had a swimming pool, and Bertha donned a two-piece wool swimsuit and a full-length robe to test the waters. Finding that everyone "in and out of the pool, except ourselves, was stark naked," Bertha indulged in what she said was one of the greatest desires of her life. She "enjoyed again the freedom of those first nine months of life when, naked, I swam in the waters of the womb."

In 1937, Bertha again left Alice behind to attend the same group's conference, this time in Edinburgh, Scotland. At a banquet honoring the visiting physicians, Bertha made what appeared to her British hosts an outrageous faux pas. To fill the lull following a toast to the king and queen, Bertha proposed a toast to the Duchess of Windsor, the American divorcee that Edward VII abdicated his throne to marry.

Bertha relished travel, and because of her reputation as a gifted surgeon, she was frequently asked to demonstrate her techniques in foreign clinics. As she aged, she was eager to see areas of her own country that she had missed, and she embarked on automobile tours of the West.

Her age was never a factor when her career and interests were concerned. At seventy, she became active in a movement to encourage mothers to breastfeed their infants, and she founded the Chicago Mother's Milk Bureau to aid women who were unable to produce milk.

Her abhorrence of smoking led her to become the vice president of the Anti-Cigarette League and the assistant editor of the *Narcotic Review*. She remembered her father's battles with his nicotine habit. Joshua would say, "I smoke once a day. I begin in the morning and stop at night." As a child, Bertha enjoyed sorting and cleaning his pipes and filling them with tobacco. When she was eight, her father experienced breathing difficulties and decided to quit. She watched him pacing in the farmhouse's yard with an empty pipe in his mouth until her mother took her away from the parlor window. "Your father is going through torture," she was told. Joshua never smoked again. Bertha was ahead of her time in her concern for the effects of secondhand smoke on children. She wrote, "Very few parents would allow their children to smoke even one cigarette a day, yet they fill the room where the children are playing or eating with a dense cloud of tobacco smoke." She advised all new patients to refrain from smoking for six months so that she could determine the habit's effect on their health.

As a young doctor newly located to Chicago, Bertha served as an emergency physician at the Columbian World's Fair. At the time, she was unaware of the efforts female doctors had to exert to get a state appropriation for a Woman's Hospital exhibit. Forty years later, female physicians again found themselves excluded from Chicago's Century of Progress International Exposition in 1933–1934. It was to take place between Twelfth and Thirty-Ninth Streets on the near south side. After convincing the event's committee to allow an exhibit on maternal hygiene, Bertha and Dr. Lena Sadler used creative fundraising techniques. By selling display space to maternity wear manufacturers, they were able to finance the booth, another on the history of women in medicine in the Hall of Social Science, and a third devoted to child welfare in another section.

In 1940, Bertha was the subject of a *Time* article explaining her unorthodox method for teaching a cesarean section technique. It described her as a "tiny, twinkling seventy-seven-year-old." Bertha displayed a manger-like box that held hand-knit replicas of pelvic organs; these enclosed a small doll in a pink silk womb. In describing her personality, the article recounted an episode when the feisty doctor insisted that the husband of a woman infected with gonorrhea stand at her side as she operated on the women's uterus. When the husband fainted, Bertha was described as saying, "Throw some water on him...He's responsible for this thing, and he is going to see it through."

Accolades continued to be bestowed on Bertha as she entered a vigorous old age. She was named by the Women's Bureau of the US Department of Labor as a representative of women's highest achievement in her field. After her retirement from teaching in 1937, she was made professor emeritus at Loyola University. Newspaper reporters followed her on her busy rounds and described her amazing energy and stamina. Her health remained strong but a bout of pneumonia brought Alice from Michigan to stay at her side. A streptococci infection caught during an abdominal operation caused her to lose the index finger of her left hand. Ever the optimist, she announced that the loss of the finger only made her hand smaller and more agile.

Among the memories of recognition Bertha received over her career, her fondest were of the dinners organized by her close friend, Dr. Lindsay Wynekoop. She met Lindsay and her husband, Frank, when all three were associated with Northwestern University Women's Medical School. At the first dinner, given in recognition of Bertha's twenty-fifth anniversary as a physician, Dr. Wynekoop had a loving cup engraved with the names of Bertha's female physician friends. At another dinner given as a farewell party before the trip to China, Dr. Wynekoop arranged for a speaker from each group and club of which Bertha was a member. Ten years later, Dr. Wynekoop held a banquet in honor of Bertha's seventieth birthday. Writing that the guests "outdid themselves in a rivalry of praise and appreciation," Bertha wrote that the most prized accolade was from her sister. Alice was unable to attend, but she wrote a tender letter to be read at the event:

> How infinitely dear to me you have always been, bone of my bone, flesh of my flesh. We have never thought of any person so much as we have of each other. We are old now, and may nothing ever mar...the unanimity that has been the sweetest thing in life...accept this as a tribute from one who has leaned on your loyalty, been strengthened by your love, been happy always in the sunshine of your optimism, who is most thankful for your existence.

With Alice in Michigan, Bertha began to lean more on Chicago friends, especially Lindsay Wynekoop. Bertha was shocked to read a November 23, 1933 headline that Wynekoop's daughter-in-law had been murdered, and Bertha's lifelong friend Lindsay was the prime suspect. The tabloids told a lurid tale of a mother's unnatural jealousy of her son's wife and painted a macabre image of the recently widowed doctor's home and private clinic. The young woman was found on the doctor's examination table in the basement of the home, chloroformed and shot after her philandering husband left the city. Out of fear for her son, Wynekoop confessed to the killing and then later recanted. Bertha watched in horror as her friend was dragged through a highly publicized trial and convicted.

Bertha developed a theory of the crime and was convinced that the girl was "accidentally shot by a deranged person." Her suspicions fell on her friend's brother-in-law, Dr. Gilbert Wynekoop. Gilbert was a morphine addict who had been accused of attempted rape by several nurses. He spent time in an insane asylum, and it was not clear if he was institutionalized at the time of the murder. Bertha visited Lindsay often in the reformatory at Dwight, Illinois, and watched her friend deteriorate into a "despairing helpless prisoner."

In 1944, Lindsay informed Bertha that she had an opportunity to petition for parole, and she needed Bertha to appear before the board. Bertha found composing her defense of Lindsay the most difficult writing she had ever done. She "wanted the gentlemen on the parole board to understand that her friend was no common person...but a medical woman." She chronicled Lindsay's education, career, philanthropy, and devotion to her family. Her request was denied, but she was successful in a second petition in 1949. Wynekoop was seventy-nine years old at the time of her release, and she died two years later, her life and reputation destroyed.

NINE

Opening the Door

The advent of World War II renewed the effort to admit female physicians to the military's commissioned ranks. Bertha was pleased that the current president of the AMWA was Emily Dunning Barringer, the first female ambulance surgeon and the first woman to receive a surgical residency. Bertha had nominated the New York physician, hoping that she would choose as her presidency's goal the acceptance of women into the armed services.

In 1940, the AMWA petitioned the AMA for support in changing the law, but the male-dominated association declined. Barringer threw herself into the contentious issue, using the AMWA membership, campaign funds, and influential friends to lobby Washington. Due to the shortage of medical personnel as the war dragged on, the government began to rethink its rejection of female physicians, and the AMA withdrew its objections.

In 1942, the US government wanted to employ female doctors only on a contract basis or confine them to the Women's Army Auxiliary Corps (WAAC). Dr. Barringer traveled to Washington to testify at the House of Representatives Committee on Military Affairs hearings held in March 1943. The medical women found an ally in the hearing's chairman, New York Congressman Emanuel Celler. Calling the War Department's interpretation of Public Law 252 "mid-Victorian," Celler explained that it "deemed that women are not persons and cannot be commissioned." He related that Dr. Barbara Stimson, a highly respected orthopedic surgeon and the cousin of the current secretary of war, had earned the rank of major in the British Royal Medical Corps after being rejected for military service in her own country. Opponents contended that female doctors were needed at home. Congressman Harness of Arizona asked if women "would render just as great a service by staying home and taking care of

103

the civil population." One congressman stated that the nation would lose the doctors who cared for children.

While the law relegated female physicians to stateside positions as members of the WAAC, the nation allowed some women into combat zones. Army nurses saw hazardous duty in the war's fiercest theaters with no commissions. "Women are welcomed in any clime where life is held precious. Why should our army be the exception?" Congressman Celler asked.

Massachusetts Democrat Philip Philbin appeared to touch on the men's greatest concern: if female doctors were commissioned, would one reach the rank of brigadier general? Celler responded that the result of commissioning women in the armed forces would be that "barriers would come down" as well as the "concern about women having a higher rank than men." He introduced petitions, letters, and telegrams supporting the acceptance of women in the armed forces and led the testimony of nineteen physicians and other concerned citizens to a successful conclusion.

Bertha and the other eight thousand practicing female physicians were vindicated when President Roosevelt signed H.R. 1857, known as the Sparkman Act, into law on April 17, 1942. The first woman to be commissioned into the Army Medical Corps, Dr. Margaret D. Craighill, was given the rank of major. Craighill, the dean of the Women's Medical College of Philadelphia, was soon followed by Dr. Eleanor Gutman, commissioned as a captain, and Dr. Elizabeth Gerber, a first lieutenant.

As the war continued, Bertha struggled to learn the fate of the surgical daughters who had become medical missionaries in China. Her feeling of responsibility for the young women who followed her into the medical field never left her, and she felt a duty to offer American girls guidance in their choice of vocation. "Lectures on vocational guidance, and even personal advice, too often fail," she wrote.

Having always been a great storyteller, Bertha began to write down her recollections of life on the farm and her experiences in medical school and as a young female physician, thinking that they would aid young women in forming their own professional goals. In 1940, she approached Florence Jameson, a friend who was an English teacher, with her accumulated notes and stories, and the two began a collaboration that became Bertha's autobiography, *Petticoat Surgeon*. Bertha envisioned the book as being written in three parts—the history of her ancestors, her own life story, and her medical stories—so that the book "might be of practical as well as biological value." She wanted to show that "happiness is found by doing the kind of work one loves and how distinction can be gained if one is willing to pay the price." Her plan was to use "symbolic drawings" by Chicago artist Mina Hoskins to illustrate the chapter headings. Hoskins produced renderings of the life cycle of the human egg, while other illustrations were to include newspaper clippings featuring Bertha and Sarah Van Hoosen Jones.

Bertha was still working on the manuscript in July 1945 when the *Chicago Daily News* published an article that followed the eighty-two-year-old surgeon on a typical workday. Photos showed Bertha leaving her home at 6:45 a.m. and operating on a patient an hour later, and the piece explained that she continued to work ten-hour days. The article ended with an image of Bertha wrapped in a robe, surrounded by books, and working on a book tentatively titled *The Cacklings of a Hen Medic*. The New York publishing house Pellegrini & Cudahy accepted the manuscript, and the book was released in 1947. The reviews were glowing. The *Chicago Daily Tribune* called it a "frank, spirited, sometimes amusing log of her sixty years in medicine." The author was cited not only for her achievements and tenacity but also for her honesty, humor, and "frankness of language."

A library in Michigan reported that a patron asked the librarian for the book "The Pantywaist Doctor."

Sales were brisk and interest high. The book garnered international attention and was translated into several languages as well as Braille. True to her original plan, *Petticoat Surgeon* took the reader through Bertha's Stoney Creek childhood, her family relationships and her experiences in education. She explained her reasoning for entering medicine and the obstacles she needed to overcome.

While chronicling the successes and frustrations of a long career, Bertha shared her life view and the words she lived by. "Every hour brings light" was the theme of much of her life story as she related the numerous times she was able to change her circumstances with hard work and perseverance. Organized religion had not played a prominent role in her life, but her profession brought her into contact with life's most traumatic events and her patients' faith response. Asked by Dr. Gunsaulus of Chicago's Armour Institute what faith she practiced, Bertha said, "I will leave it to you. Last week, on Sunday, I baptized an unborn child of Catholic parents, because its life was in danger. On Wednesday, I was the only woman attending a Jewish circumcision, the parents refusing to have the *mohel* operate without my presence. On Friday, with a tiny casket in my arms, I went alone to the cemetery with the body of a baby whose parents did not believe in funerals." She dedicated the last portion of her book to the tragic story of Dr. Lindsay Wynekoop and wrote that she called on God to help her lifelong friend.

Bertha admitted that she had no belief in an afterlife and did not fear death. She believed that "to die is as natural as to be born, that without death birth would become a greater tragedy than death could ever be." She continued to believe that a woman could have a fulfilling career and marry. She wrote that she regretted her "spat" with the handsome young Latin professor at the University of Michigan. When honored by the University of Chicago alumnae club of Chicago at a dinner in 1948, Bertha was asked why she never married. She had to admit that she hadn't been asked, but she also explained that the men of her day would not have been as accepting of a professional wife as she believed modern men were.

She wrote extensively about the family she had created. She was so pleased that Alice, Sarah, and herself were "independent in our own spheres and yet so dependent on each other." Bertha wrote with great pride about Sarah's success on the Michigan farm. "No father has ever gloated more over any laurels bestowed upon his offspring," she wrote.

The bestselling book brought further invitations to speak and travel. On a 1947 trip to London with Sarah, Bertha bragged of her niece's driving skill and ability to change not one but two tires on one afternoon's ride. A visit to her Danish publisher and an address in Stockholm involved her first airplane ride, and she announced herself to be "quite an airplane fan."

In an excited letter to Alice and Sarah in Michigan, Bertha shared the news that she had been made an honorary member of the International Medical Women's Association. "I am the only honorary member except Marie Curie. These are certainly times with so many ups and downs that one day I am weeping and the next shouting." Her frustrations stemmed from her efforts to create a medical women's library on the campus of the Women's Medical School of Pennsylvania, the last women-only medical school in the United States. Bertha dreamed that the building would also provide a headquarters for the American Medical Women's Association. AMWA members formed a committee to organize a collection of books "by or about medical women; scrapbooks with press notices relating to medical, dental, and allied science women" that Bertha started years before. The oversized book on maternal hygiene that had been exhibited at the 1930 Century of Progress International Exposition was being held at the Rosenwald Museum of Science and Industry in anticipation of the library's opening.

In celebration of the medical school's centennial, Bertha wanted to have the library and Blackwell Memorial Hall completed by 1950. She set about to raise $500,000 and spent what political capital she had soliciting funds. Former First Lady Eleanor Roosevelt responded to a letter from Bertha with an offer to have her name be associated with the library but no money. Blackwell Teas, gatherings named for America's first women doctor, were held to collect donations. Bertha asked for "large gifts" for the library fund to complete "the only memorial hall in the world rendering homage to women." Her publisher agreed to send one dollar to the fund for each autographed copy of *Petticoat Surgeon* they sold. Unable to reach her fundraising goal, Bertha offered to name the library after Myrtle Walgreen if the wife of the drugstore entrepreneur would cover the construction. In 1949, she related planning to make a "phonograph record on smoking that I hope to sell to benefit the medical women's library." The proposed library's collection was housed in the University of Chicago Medical School's Quine Library on Polk Street as Bertha continued her efforts to raise the needed money.

Sarah later wrote that friends asked Bertha when she would retire. Sarah reported that Bertha told them "I do not know. Fate will decide for me." In February 1950, Sarah let Bertha know that her older sister, Alice, had fallen and broken her hip. Now ninety-five, Alice had given up her life in Chicago to accompany her daughter to Michigan. She had organized Sarah's home as she had the home she shared with Bertha. Bertha took a night train to Detroit and stood nearby as Alice underwent surgery.

Bertha made her retirement decision: Alice needed her. She would not return to live in Chicago but stay by her sister's side.

Arrangements were made to leave her medical practice with her partner and move her belongings to Stoney Creek. The sisters shared what had been the front parlor in their childhood home. Mornings were spent seeing to Alice's needs, clearing the kitchen, and preparing for the noon meal. While Alice dozed in the afternoon, Bertha wrote letters to friends and solicitations for the memorial library fund. She attended to a few local patients and operated on a woman with a cancerous breast after moving to Michigan. When the doctor who had taken over her Stoney Creek practice in 1940 wanted time off for a honeymoon, Bertha saw some of her clients.

Alice was a difficult patient. In a letter to a surgical daughter, Bertha complained, "It gets harder and harder to get anything to please her." Bertha felt that Alice should try to do some exercise, and for a time, Alice moved around the first floor of the house with the aid of a walker. Finally, she refused to leave her bed and began to fail mentally. She stared out the window for hours at a time and failed to recognize her devoted sister. When Alice died later that year, she was laid to rest in the pioneer cemetery above the village, joining her mother and father.

Soon after her mother's death, Sarah sought to reconnect with her half-brother, Horton. Now a retired mining engineer, he lived in Tomball, Texas, with his wife, a retired teacher. Sarah located him while on a speaking engagement, and she reported her find to Bertha. Bertha wholeheartedly approved of the brother-sister reunion. The siblings provided funds for their father's grave in Adrian, Michigan, and remained in touch until Horton's death in 1969.

After moving into one of the upstairs bedrooms, Bertha settled into a quiet routine. Still fundraising for the library, she spent many hours writing letters and teaching herself to type using a "hunt-and-peck" system. She obtained a hearing aid in 1950 and started to complain of physical ailments. In a letter to surgical daughter, Rose Mendian, she reported needing to wear a corset to bed to relieve back pain, though she had always disapproved of their use. Writing to "My Dearest Rose Child" and signing off as "your miserable loving surgical mother," Bertha mentioned looking into booking passage on the *RMS Queen Elizabeth* but being "leery about being well enough to go." She was content to spend mornings writing and helping with small household chores while Sarah spent time at the dairy barn. Semiretired, Sarah took Bertha for afternoon rides around the countryside and visited relatives and friends nearby. In the fall of 1951, Bertha wrote, "The fall is lovely here and getting more wonderful every day. I am very happy here with my niece, and the neighbors are lovely to me."

Returning to the farmhouse from an errand late in October, Sarah found her aunt on the floor of the kitchen, unable to move. A stroke had paralyzed her left side. Immobile and with diminished mental ability, Bertha was moved to a convalescent home in Bruce Township, north of the farm. Sarah and her employee and family friend, Alice Serrell took turns spending hours at her bedside. Bertha survived seven months before she joined Alice and their parents in the pioneer cemetery.

Obituaries called Bertha the world's oldest and most well-known female physician. She was hailed for her surgical skill, work ethic, and empathy for her patients. Former students and surgical daughters praised her knowledge, ability, and inspiring teaching.

Bertha best described how she would be remembered when she wrote near the end of her life: "When I was born, the door that separates the sexes had opened scarcely more than a crack. And it has been my privilege, my pain, and my pleasure to pound on that door, strain at its hinges and finally to see it, although not wide open, stand ajar."

Epilogue

A lone for the first time in her life, Sarah Jones asked Alice Serrell to move into the Van Hoosen farmhouse that she had shared with her mother and aunt. The friends lived an active retirement. They made multiple round-the-world trips, sharing the photos they took with local ladies' groups. Sarah was an active citizen who served on numerous boards and was often referred to as "Mrs. Rochester." She appreciated that her aunt was an historical figure and made a gift of Bertha Van Hoosen's numerous papers to the Bentley Historical Library at the University of Michigan–Ann Arbor. A large portion of her self-published memoir, *Chronicle of Van Hoosen Centenary Farm*, was dedicated to the pioneering surgeon.

When Sarah died in 1972, she left her personal belongings, "deemed to have no historic significance," and a $100,000 trust to her companion, Alice Serrell. The remainder of her estate—the Van Hoosen farmhouse, the farm buildings, 350 acres of farm, and several Stoney Creek Village homes—was left to Michigan State University. Sarah had had a close relationship with Michigan's former agricultural college and served several terms on its board. Her will stipulated that the estate be used "in such a manner as it shall deem to be in the best interest of said Michigan State University." She also asked that Serrell be allowed to live in the farmhouse as long as she wished.

In 1979, a petition was begun by a local group of Questors, an international organization interested in historic preservation. The petition asked that Michigan State University donate back three and a half acres, including the Van Hoosen farmhouse, to Avon Township with the stipulation that it be developed as a museum. Serrell continued to live in the house until she moved to Florida in 1982. Over time, the university sold the rest of the homes and acreage that Sarah had bequeathed. The

Van Hoosen barns and twelve acres were purchased from a developer for use in the museum complex.

The Rochester Hills Museum at Van Hoosen Farm was opened to the public in 1984. It celebrates the extraordinary lives of the members of the Van Hoosen family, especially the "petticoat surgeon," Bertha Van Hoosen.

All illustrations used with permission of the Rochester Hills Museum at Van Hoosen Farm.

Bibliography

"A Petticoat Surgeon and Her Memoirs." *Chicago Daily Tribune,* Aug. 24, 1947.

A University of MichiganChronology:http://bentley.umich.edu/exhibits/umtimeline/general.php

Bellamy, Edward. *Looking Backward.* New York: Buccaneer Books, 1888.

Certificate of Marriage. General Registry Office. London.

Chapman, Charles C. History of Michigan. Chicago: Chas. C. Chapman, 1881.

Cooke Mills, James. *History of Saginaw County.* Saginaw: Seemann & Peters, 1918.

Edwards, Jim. *Chicago's Opulent Age 1870s–1840s in Vintage Postcards.* Chicago: Arcadia Publishing, 2001.

Journal of Social History 15, no. 4 (1982): 607–19.

Lemons, J. Stanley. *The Woman Citizen: Social Feminism in the 1920s.* Charlottesville, VA: University of Virginia Press, 1990.

Loyola University of Chicago Archives. *Journal of the American Medical Women's Association* 12 (1957): 22–24.

McGuigan, Dorothy Gies. *Dangerous Experiment: 100 Years of Women at the University of Michigan.* Ann Arbor: Center for Continuing Education of Women, 1970.

Medical News Journal of the American Med Assoc. 1922; 79 (19): 1615–1621Olson, Avis M. Bertha Van Hoosen, M.D. (1863-1952). *Journal of the American Medical Women's Association*18, no7 (1963)

Mendian, Rose V. "A Surgical Daughter's Impressions." *Journal of the American Medical Women's Association* 20 (1965): 349–50.

"Oldest Woman Doctor Dies in Michigan Home." *Chicago Daily Tribune,* June 8, 1952.

Olson, Avis M. Bertha Van Hoosen, M.D. (1863-1952). *Journal of the American Medical Association* 18, no7 (1963)

Saginaw Schools Illustrated Quarterly 1, no. 1 (1977).

"Still on the Job at 82." *Chicago Daily News*, July 14, 1945.

Sophia Smith Collection. Smith College Archives, New England Hospital Collection.

The Chicago Metro History Education Center: Chicago History Fair: Women's History Topics.

The University of Michigan and China: 1845–2008. Edited by Nancy Bartlett. Ann Arbor, MI: Bentley Historical Library, 2007.

United States Congress, House Committee on Military Affairs, Hearings before Subcommittee No. 3 of the Committee on Military Affairs, House of Representatives (March 10, 11, and 18), 1943.

Van Hoosen, Bertha. Medical Women's National Association-Reasons for Its Existence-Its Scope and Its Work. *The Medical Women's Journal* 26 (April 1916): 97-98

Van Hoosen, Bertha. *Petticoat Surgeon.* Unpublished manuscript. Bentley Historical Library, Ann Arbor.

Van Hoosen, Bertha. *Petticoat Surgeon.* Chicago: Pellegrini & Cudahy, 1947.

Van Hoosen, Bertha and Elizabeth Ross Shaw. Scopolamine-Morphine Anesthesia. Chicago: The House of Manz, 1915.

Van Hoosen, Bertha. Traveling through the Orient. *The Medical Woman's Journal* 30 (Nov. 1923): 336–45.

Van Hoosen, Bertha. Traveling through the Orient. *The Medical Woman's Journal* 30 (Dec. 1923): 371–75.

Van Hoosen Jones Papers. Bentley Historical Library, Ann Arbor.

Van Hoosen Jones, Sarah. *Chronicle of Van Hoosen Centenary Farm.* 1969.

Women Building Chicago 1790–1990: A Biographical Dictionary. Edited by Rima Lunin Schultz and Adele Hast. Bloomington, IN: Indiana University Press, 2001.

Index

Page numbers in italics refer to images.

Jones, Edward Horton, 16, 17, 24, 26, *30*,
    43, 47, 108
Jones, Eliphalet, 15
Jones, Elisha, 15–16
Jones, Joseph Comstock, 24; life of,
    15–16; Alice boards with, 17;
    courtship and marriage of, 25–26;
    in farmhouse parlor, *30*; and birth of
    Sarah Jones, 34; career change of, 34,
    37; financial troubles of, 42–43; as
    father and husband, 43;
    death of, 47
Jones, Lydia Field, 15
Jones, Myra, 24, 26
Jones, Nettie, 16, 17, 24
Jones, Sarah Van Hoosen: following
    death of Sarah Van Hoosen, 1; circa
    1892, *30*; birth of, 33–34; Alice's
    worries regarding, 37; upbringing
    of, 43; diagnosed with malaria
    and diabetes insipidus, 48–49;
    personality of, 55; tours Europe,
    55–57; with Alice, *60*; in Scotland,
    61; with family, *63*; on family
    dinner conversation, 65; education
    of, 75–76; returns to Stoney Creek
    farm, 75–76; at University of
    Wisconsin–Madison, *86*; circa
    1933, *87*; runs farm, 95–96; Bertha's
    relationship with, 106; reunites
    with brother Horton, 108; and
    Bertha's final years,109; final years
    and estate of, 111
Journal of the American Medical
    Association (JAMA), 58

Kahn, Ida, 80–81
Kalamazoo State Hospital, 32
Kobe, Japan, 84–86
Kwangtung Medical School, 79–80

Lewis, Allen Cleveland, 42
Lewis Institute, 42
Lister, Joseph, 31
Looking Backward (Bellamy), 46
Loyola University School of Medicine,
    73–74, 93

Mahan, Patrick, 72–73
male patients, 68
marriage, 93–94, 106
Martin, Emma, 82
Mary Institute, 20–21
Mary Thompson Hospital, 45, *88*
Mayo Clinic, 53
McCormick, Alexander, 79
McLean, Donald, 23
McLean, Mary, 18–19, 20–22, 35,
    60, 78
Medical Woman's Journal, The, 58, 72
Medical Women's National Association
    (MWNA), 70–71
mentoring, 67
Mergler, Marie, 36
Michigan State University, 96, 111
Moorehead, Louis D., 72–73, 74
Morton, Rosalie Slaughter, 71

New England Hospital for Women, 32,
    33–34
New Zealand, 79

tobacco, 99

travel, 25, 55–57, 77–83, 97–99, 106

tree, community giving, 8

T'sao, Li Yuin, 81

twilight sleep, 57–58. *See also*
scopolamine-morphine anesthesia

typhoid fever, 32

University of Michigan–Ann Arbor:
female enrollment at, 12–13; Alice
graduates from, 15; Bertha attends,
17–18, 22–23; Bertha teaches anatomy
at, 24–25, 31–32; relationship with
Chinese government, 77–78

Van Hoosen, Alice: birth of, 4; Bertha's
relationship with, 6–7, 17, 31–32, 95,
101, 106; education of, 8–11;
enrolls in University of
Michigan, 13; college graduation
of, 15; employment of, 15, 16, 17, 18;
courtship and marriage of, 25–26;
circa 1869, 28; circa 1880, 29; in
farmhouse parlor, 30; gives birth to
Sarah Jones, 33–34; worries
over baby and finances, 37;
correspondence between Joseph
Jones and, 43; summers in Stoney
Creek, 43–44; role of, in Bertha's
private practice, 48; bias of, against
women doctors, 48–49; cares for
Sarah during illness, 49;
tours Europe, 55–57, 97–98; with
Sarah, 60; in North Africa, 62; with
family, 63; daily life of, in
Chicago, 65; as suffragist, 67; as

mother, 75; returns to Stoney Creek
farm, 76; illness of, in China, 83;
following Great Kanto Earthquake,
84–85; with Bertha in Stoney Creek,
88; life of, on farm, 96, 97; final years
and death of, 107–8

Van Hoosen, Bertha, *63*, *88*; birth of, 4;
education of, 5–6, 8–12, 15, 17–18;
childhood of, 5–8; kindness of, 8;
chooses medical career, 18–20;
decides on medical career, 18–20;
medical education of, 20–25;
circa 1869, *28*; circa 1880, *29*; at
University of Michigan, *29*; circa
1889, *30*; in farmhouse parlor, *30*;
as head of house, 47–48, 67, 75, 95;
appearance of, 48; dedication of, to
career, 48; skill and presentation
of, 54; with Mary McClean, *60*;
performing surgery, *61*; in 1910, *62*;
in North Africa, *62*; with family, *63*;
with Alice in Stoney Creek, *88*; at
Chicago Women's Club, *88*; at Mary
Thompson Hospital, *88*; personality
of, 100; accolades and recognition
for, 100–101; final years and death of,
108–9; life of, ix–x

Van Hoosen, Joshua Jr., *27*; ancestry and
early years of, 2–3; courtship and
marriage of, 3–4; industriousness
and livelihood of, 4–5; Bertha's
relationship with, 5; on religion, 7;
on Santa Claus, 8; lack of refinement
in, 9; takes Alice and Bertha to and
from school, 10; Bertha lies to, 11;
unable to support Bertha's medical

Made in the USA
San Bernardino, CA
15 September 2016